BEGINNING
ILLUSTRATION AND
STORYBOARDING
FOR GAMES

Beginning Illustration and Storyboarding for Games

Les Pardew

THOMSON

™

COURSE TECHNOLOGY

Professional ■ Trade ■ Reference

ISBN: 1-59200-495-4
Library of Congress Catalog Card Number: 2004108016
Printed in the United States of America
04 05 06 07 08 BH 10 9 8 7 6 5 4 3 2 1

SVP, Thomson Course Technology PTR:
Andy Shafran

Publisher:
Stacy L. Hiquet

Senior Marketing Manager:
Sarah O'Donnell

Marketing Manager:
Heather Hurley

Manager of Editorial Services:
Heather Talbot

Acquisitions Editor:
Mitzi Koontz

Senior Editor:
Mark Garvey

Associate Marketing Managers:
Kristin Eisenzopf and
Sarah Dubois

Project Editor/Copy Editor:
Cathleen D. Snyder

Course Technology PTR Market Coordinator:
Elizabeth Furbish

Interior Layout Tech:
Scribe Tribe

Cover Designer:
Mike Tanamachi

CD-ROM Producer:
Brandon Penticuff

Indexer:
Sharon Shock

Proofreader:
Kim V. Benbow

THOMSON

COURSE TECHNOLOGY

Professional ■ Trade ■ Reference
Thomson Course Technology PTR,
a division of Thomson Course Technology
25 Thomson Place
Boston, MA 02210
http://www.courseptr.com

To all the art teachers and mentors I have had over the years, I dedicate this book. I have learned from many, some of whom don't even know that they were my instructors. Those who have spent time working with me to develop my artistic talents are and always will be great in my eyes.

I also dedicate this book to all the young artists who will make a difference in the time to come. May you always have faith in your work and love for art. I pray God's blessing on each of you.

ACKNOWLEDGMENTS

This book has been an effort of much work, and I thank all those who have helped. Especially, I thank my wife, Kim, for her unfailing faith in her artist husband, and my children, for the time that they let me have to write. I thank my parents, who have always believed in me. I also thank my editor, who has had to put up with an artist's writing ability.

I also thank the many artists and friends who have contributed to the book. I appreciate the contributions in artwork, encouragement, and knowledge.

About the Author

In 1987, **Les Pardew** started his career by creating the animation for *Magic Johnson Fast Break Basketball* on the Commodore 64. He soon found that he loved working on games and has been in the industry ever since. His work encompasses more than 100 video game titles, including some major titles such as *Super Star Wars*, *NCAA Basketball*, *Starcraft: Brood War*, *James Bond 007*, *Robin Hood: Prince of Thieves*, and *CyberTiger*. He currently serves as President of Alpine Studios, which he founded with Ross Wolfley in the fall of 2000. Alpine Studios is a game development company focusing on family-friendly games. Alpine Studios' products include *Kublox*, *Combat Medic*, *Motocross Mania 2*, and *Ford Truck Mania*. Les is also the author of *Game Art for Teens*.

Contents

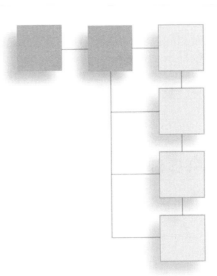

Introduction . . . . **xv**

Chapter 1   **Basic Game Design Art** **1**

Art Used in Game Designs. 1

   Game Layout Charts 2

   Storyboards 3

   Level Layouts 6

   Environment Illustrations 7

   Character Designs 8

   Model Sheets. 10

   Graphical User Interface Design. 11

   Other Concept Art. 12

Summary 13

Questions 13

Answers. 14

Discussion Questions 15

Exercises 15

Chapter 2   **Creating Game Layout Charts** **17**

Designing the Style of the Chart. 17

Building the Game Layout Chart. 19

Building the Second Page of the Game Layout Chart. 26

Other Types of Level Designs. 31

Charting Complex Games 35

Summary 36

Questions 37

Answers. 37

Discussion Questions 38

Exercises 38

Chapter 3   **The Thumbnail Sketch** **39**

Drawing. 39

The Paper 40

The Pencil 41

Drawing Technique 42

Pencil Strokes 44

Creating the Thumbnail Sketch. 46

Character Thumbnails 48

Design Tool. 50

Summary. 51

Questions 52

Answers. 52

Discussion Questions 53

Exercises 53

Chapter 4   **The Storyboard** **55**

Creating Games Takes Time and Money. 55

Games Can Be Difficult to Explain 56

Storyboarding Helps with Communication 56

Storyboarding Aids in Problem Solving 57

What Are Storyboards Used for in Games? 57

Cinematic Sequences. 57

Animation. 58

Complexity 58

Non-Player Actions 59

Are Storyboards Important? 59

Learning about Storyboards 59

    Camera Direction. 61

    Written Directions. 65

    Special-Use Panels 65

Showing Action 67

Summary 68

Questions 69

Answers. 69

Discussion Questions 70

Exercises 70

Chapter 5   **Drawing Storyboards** **71**

Basic Drawing Skills 71

    Perspective 72

    Composition. 78

    Balance 78

    Focal Points 81

    Pathways. 84

    Shading. 84

Creating the Storyboard 87

Summary 92

Questions 93

Answers. 94

Discussion Questions 94

Exercises 94

Chapter 6   **Level Layouts** **95**

What Are Level Layouts? 95

How Level Layouts Are Used in Game Creation. 96

    Creating Level Designs 96

    Determining Asset Count 98

    Defining the Story 99

Placing Characters and Objects 99

Placing Events 99

Defining Paths 99

Information in Level Layouts................................... 100

Creating a Level Layout 101

Summary... 108

Questions 108

Answers.. 109

Discussion Questions 109

Exercises 110

Chapter 7   Illustrating Environments **111**

What Is an Environment Illustration?........................... 111

Uses and Purposes of Environment Illustrations 111

Inspiration 112

Direction... 112

Creating an Environment Sketch............................... 113

Using Color 118

How Light Affects Colors 118

Using the Color Wheel 120

Creating an Environment Illustration 123

Summary... 129

Questions 130

Answers.. 130

Discussion Questions 131

Exercises 131

Chapter 8   Quick Character Sketches **133**

Game Characters 133

Types of Game Characters..................................... 134

Player Characters 134

Non-Player Characters 135

Enemies.. 135

Getting Ideas for Characters 136

Drawing Characters 137

Why Quick Sketches? 137

Drawing the Head 138

Drawing the Full Figure 140

Character Exaggeration 144

Non-Human Characters 146

Summary 149

Questions 149

Answers 150

Discussion Questions 150

Exercises 151

Chapter 9 **Creating Character Illustrations** **153**

Character Illustrations 153

How Are Character Illustrations Used? 154

What Makes a Good Character Illustration? 155

Simple Character Illustrations 155

Detailed Character Illustrations 162

Summary 168

Questions 169

Answers 169

Discussion Questions 170

Exercises 170

Chapter 10 **Creating Character Model Sheets** **171**

What Are Model Sheets? 171

How Are Model Sheets Used? 173

Creating Base Model Sheets 175

The Male Character 176

The Female Character 178

Creating the Template 180

Making Character Model Sheets 181

Color in Model Sheets 184

Summary 185

Questions 186

Answers. 186

Discussion Questions 187

Exercises 187

Chapter 11   Designing Graphical User Interfaces 189

What Are Graphical User Interfaces? 189

Information Screens 189

Menus. 194

Onscreen Displays 197

Creating Game Navigation Design 200

Creating Onscreen Elements 204

Summary 209

Questions 209

Answers. 210

Discussion Questions 210

Exercises 210

Chapter 12   The Design Document 211

Understanding Design Documents. 211

The Design Document as a Repository 212

The Design Document as a Roadmap 212

The Design Document as a Promotion Tool 213

Developing Themes 213

Designing Covers 215

Designing Title Pages. 217

Working with Fonts 219

Readability 219

Style 220

Page Layout 222

Layout Styles. 222

Formal. 223

Diagonal 224

Staggered. 225

Flush 226

Two-Column Flush. 227

Two-Column Random 228

Other Styles 229

Special Page-Layout Considerations 229

Summary 229

Questions 229

Answers. 230

Discussion Questions 231

Exercises 231

Appendix A   Concept Art in 3D 233

Building a Game Board 233

Texturing the Game Board 239

Adding the Game Pieces 250

Rendering the Game Board. 254

Index 267

INTRODUCTION

The creative work involved in creating concept art for games is one of the most rewarding jobs that an artist can have. In fact, it is possibly the most creative job in the entire game industry. Concept artists have the opportunity to visualize things that have never been seen before. They create the visual design of games. It is a huge responsibility and yet one of the most enjoyable experiences an artist can have.

When an artist creates a game, there is much more going on than in almost any other type of art anywhere. In a game, the artist is creating a self-contained world in which characters can interact with each other and things can happen. Unlike painting a picture, creating art for a game is about as close to intelligent art creation as an artist can get. It is like creating a world, and it is exciting to think about.

Concept art is the foundation of game creation. Game development relies on the concept art to give direction to the development team. The concept artist supplies the vision for the game. Without the concept art, there is a good chance that there will be miscommunication in the development process. The concept artist is the one who visualizes the game and then gives that vision to the rest of the development team.

This book is about creating game concept art. It covers a vast array of art required in the conceptual stage of game development. It is a beginning book, so it takes a basic look at creating game concept art. You do not need to have any game art development experience to read this book.

This book contains several step-by-step examples for you. These examples are designed to help you understand how the art is created. You are encouraged to follow the examples to get a feel for the project. After trying the examples in the book, you should try a few projects of your own.

Creating game concept art is fun. This book should help you on your way to a wonderful experience in creativity.

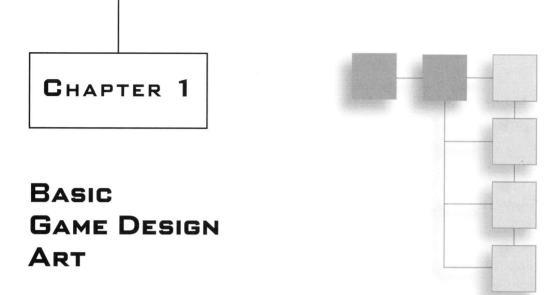

CHAPTER 1

BASIC
GAME DESIGN
ART

One of the most highly sought after jobs in the game industry is the concept artist. The concept artist is responsible for designing the visual aspects of the game, and works hand-in-hand with the game designer to craft the foundation upon which the game will be created. This foundation is called the *game design*, and it is the document that defines all of the aspects of a game. It is similar in nature to an architect's blueprint of a complex building. The game design contains detailed descriptions of the characters, settings, story, game play, and technology. It also contains extensive amounts of art.

In a game design, graphics are usually the first thing that a publisher or investor sees. The better the design's graphics, the more likely the publisher or investor will be to have a favorable impression of the design. Great concept art can often mean the difference between a design being read or ignored.

This book is a hands-on approach for the beginning artist to learn how to create concept art for game designs. It includes many step-by-step examples and a number of samples from game designs. The book is designed as a learning tool to help beginners explore the creation of concept art.

Art Used in Game Designs

Game designs include extensive amounts of art to help the game developers create the final game. Some of the art typically found in a game design includes

- Game layout charts
- Storyboards
- Level layouts
- Environment illustrations

1

- Character designs
- Model sheets
- GUI designs

I will cover each of these areas of the game design in detail in the course of this book. For now, I'll provide you with a quick look at each one so you will understand what role they have in the game design.

Game Layout Charts

The first task for the concept artist and the game designer is to lay out the game in a *game layout chart*. This chart is a visual representation of the game, showing how it will be played and all of its components (see Figure 1.1). Although the chart is a simple diagram of the game, it can become very complex.

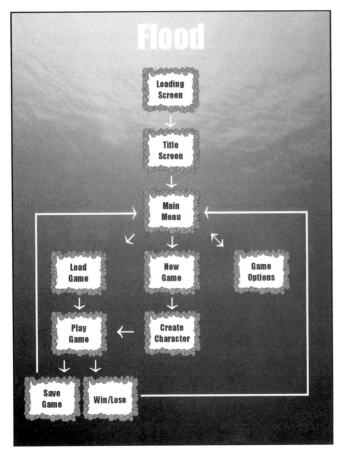

Figure 1.1
The chart shows the layout of a simple game.

The purpose of the chart is to help the development team understand how the game goes together. This is particularly important when game development involves a large team. As games continue to become more complex, the number of developers per team increases. Sometimes the team members work in different locations. The game layout chart is a simple way for the members of the team to understand the game and how each part will fit into the finished product.

The concept artist typically is not responsible for designing the content of the game layout chart (in other words, what goes into each individual panel). Instead, the artist's role is to take the information and arrange it into an understandable chart. As with everything in a game design, the chart should reflect the nature of the game.

The game layout chart is the framework upon which the concept artist will define the visual elements of the game design. Often the game design chart will include miniature versions of the finished illustrations linked to the actual pictures.

Storyboards

Storyboards are series of sketches that indicate how sequences of events should take place. In a way, they are similar to cartoon panels because they have pictures with captions explaining the scene and any possible dialogue. In games, storyboards are used to show how the game will work (see Figure 1.2).

Player chooses course at the room of doors.

Figure 1.2
The storyboard shows possible events in a game.

Unlike film and video productions, games are not linear in nature, and seldom do events occur in exactly the same way each time the game is played. Camera angles, character positions, and even outcomes will differ because the player is in control of one or more elements in the game. Therefore, storyboards for games are not used in the same way as storyboards for film and video.

A storyboard in a game design will show a possible sequence of events. The development team will use it as a guide for setting up an event. Sometimes the storyboard will need to include several possible outcomes for an event, depending on how pivotal the event is in the overall scheme of the game (see Figure 1.3).

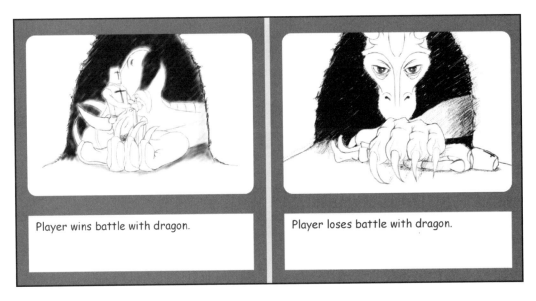

Player wins battle with dragon.

Player loses battle with dragon.

Figure 1.3
Game storyboards show possible outcomes for game events.

Storyboards in game designs are also used to show *game navigation*—the process of moving through the game (see Figure 1.4). Navigation is usually accomplished via a *user interface*, which includes all the elements that are used to control the game, such as input devices (game controllers or a mouse) and onscreen elements (buttons, menus, windows, and so on). User interfaces also include onscreen information elements, such as score, health, time, or any other important information a player needs to effectively play a game. Because games require player input to progress from one part to another, the design team needs to communicate how this navigation will be accomplished. Storyboards are a great way to show how the navigation system in a game will work.

Storyboards are also used to define cinematic sequences in a game. Often story elements in a game are developed by using short cinematic sequences (see Figure 1.5). These sequences

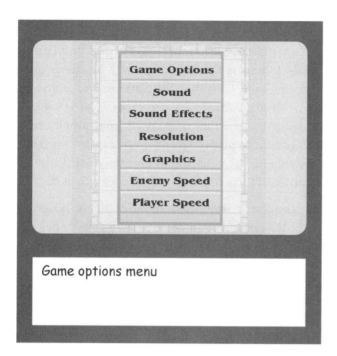

Figure 1.4
Storyboards are used to show game navigation.

are linear video clips, and they are often as sophisticated as any motion picture. They form a vital part of many games. Concept artists work with the game designer to visualize each cinematic sequence. It is the responsibility of the concept artist to create storyboards that show how a cinematic sequence will work in the game. Sometimes the artist will work with a screenwriter to develop the sequences. For cinematic sequences, the storyboards are very similar to those used in motion pictures and television.

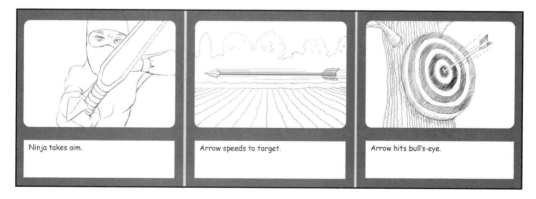

Figure 1.5
Storyboards are also used for cinematic sequences in games.

Level Layouts

Games are often broken up into levels. The term *level* has its roots in the beginning of game development, when games were restricted by technology and could have only a limited number of graphics loaded in the game at any one time. Each time the player moved from one area to another, the old graphics had to be eliminated and new graphics had to be loaded. Therefore, games were broken up into areas. Usually they progressed from simple areas to more complex ones as the player learned how to play the game. In this system of game advancement, the play areas became known as *levels*, referring to the level of difficulty in each game area. Today, the term has broadened to include any unique area in a game.

Level layouts are drawings created by the concept artist to show all the elements in a game level. These elements include a map of the terrain and all interactive characters or objects within the level (see Figure 1.6). Often these layouts are drawn to scale on grid paper or with the use of a grid in a digital drawing program.

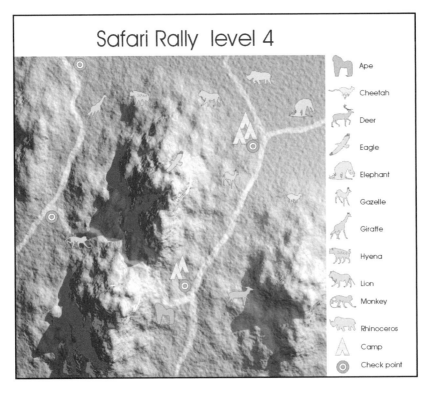

Figure 1.6
Level layouts show the terrain and interactive elements of a game area.

Level layouts often look like maps. In reality, they are maps of the game. They show where a player will start in the game area and how he can progress through the area. Sometimes the progression will take a specific path with a definite beginning and ending position on the layout, but other games use a more open system in which there are multiple entry and exit points to the level.

Environment Illustrations

An important part of a game design is the environment illustration. *Environment illustrations* are full-color illustrations of a game environment as it will be seen in the game. They are usually in the game design document with the level layouts to show the development team how the game should look. The concept artist will select important areas in a game and create illustrations that are then referenced on the level layout.

Environment illustrations help the concept artist communicate to the development team the feeling and mood of an area. They are used to show color schemes, as well as greater detail in critical areas that is not possible in the level layout (see Figure 1.7). Concept artists should use care in choosing what areas are illustrated so that each one serves a vital purpose in the development of the game.

Figure 1.7
Environment illustrations show greater detail for a specific level location.

Character Designs

One of the most common tasks a concept artist will be called on to accomplish is the creation of a character design. A *character design* is a sketch of a character that will appear in a game. *Characters* are people or creatures in a game that are controlled either by the player or through artificial intelligence. Some characters play major roles in the game and some play minor ones, but each character needs to be designed (see Figure 1.8).

Figure 1.8
Every character in a game needs to be designed.

The process of designing characters can sometimes be extensive, with the concept artist creating multiple sketches before coming up with just the right design for the game. Once a character design is chosen, the artist will usually create a detailed color rendering of the character. The rendering will become part of the design document and in some instances will be used to promote the game (see Figure 1.9).

Characters in a game are valuable intellectual property, particularly if the game becomes popular. Several game characters, such as Lara Croft and Mario, have gone on to become

Figure 1.9
Character designs are sometimes used to promote the game.

public icons. A character's name and image can be trademarked, and the concept artist's design is usually submitted to the trademark office for the trademark.

Character designs can sometimes become quite detailed (see Figure 1.10). Of all of the work a concept artist does, character designs tend to be the most widely used for other purposes.

Figure 1.10
Character designs can sometimes become quite detailed.

Model Sheets

A *model sheet* is an orthographic, detailed drawing of a character or object used by the development team to create the character or object. Model sheets are like drafting plans in that they show multiple views of the character. Most include front and back views of a character (see Figure 1.11). Some model sheets also include side and top views, particularly if the character is a quadruped.

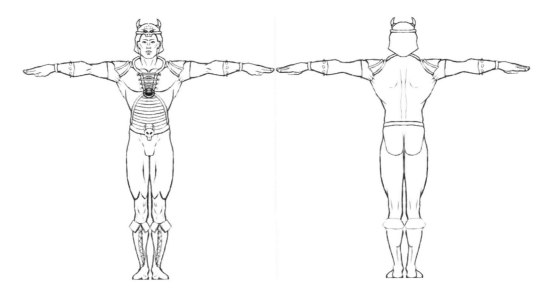

Figure 1.11
Most model sheets include front and back views of the character.

Model sheets are often used in the creation of a 3D model of the character (see Figure 1.12). They are loaded as a template for the modeler to use as a guide for creating the geometry of the character.

A game design can include multiple model sheets, one for each character in the game. Sometimes model sheets are created for important objects in a game. These objects are usually items that are critical to progress in the game or to the look of the game. A good rule in game design is to create a model sheet of any object that plays an important role in the game.

In some games, the main character will change as the game progresses. For example, many role-playing games allow the main character to change armor and weapons during the course of the game. These games require multiple model sheets for the main character.

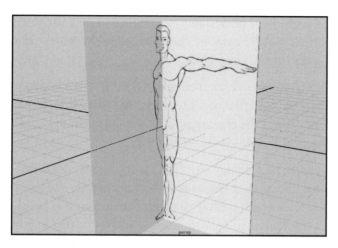

Figure 1.12
Model sheets are used in the creation of 3D models.

Graphical User Interface Design

The GUI (*Graphical User Interface*) is made up of the onscreen game elements that are used to give the player information or allow him to navigate through the game. Because these game elements are often present throughout the game, they need to be designed carefully. The GUI needs to perform a function and, at the same time, it needs to be cohesive with the design of the game (see Figure 1.13). Sometimes the GUI is as important to the mood and feel of the game as the rest of the game art is.

Figure 1.13
The GUI plays an important role in the look and feel of the game.

Some games, such as role-playing games, have very elaborate, complex GUIs. In these games, the player has to manage multiple game elements. The more game elements that a player has to manage, the more complex the GUI can become.

Good GUI design is critical to the game. A good GUI can often mean the difference between whether or not a game is a success. The concept artist needs to remember that while menus and buttons are part of the game, they are not the entire game. If the GUI is cumbersome or detracts from the core of the game play, it needs to be redesigned.

An important part of GUI design is the *heads-up display*—or HUD, as it is sometimes called. The HUD is comprised of all the onscreen interface elements present during normal game play. This display is primarily used to give the player critical game information, such as health status or the current score. In many games it is on display constantly and is updated in real time. HUDs are tricky to design because they must look nice while remaining unobtrusive to the rest of the game. They usually occupy the edges of the screen to allow the main play action to take center stage (see Figure 1.14).

Figure 1.14
The HUD occupies the areas near the edges of the screen.

Other Concept Art

Some game designs require the concept artist to create other specialized concept art. For example, a racing game might have vehicles instead of characters. A flight simulator might have specialized encounter maps that deal with only limited amounts of ground terrain. A puzzle game might require solution charts.

There is no standard format for game designs because games vary so greatly. The purpose of the game design document is to communicate the nature and extent of the game. It gives the development team and other interested parties, such as the marketing team and the management team, a clear picture of the game. Each design needs to be customized to be as clear and easy to follow as possible. The concept artist plays a critical role in its creation. So much of a game is visual in nature that it would be difficult to have a game design without the concept artist.

Summary

This chapter provided a quick overview of the types of art used in a game design. In this chapter, you should have learned the following concepts:

- Concept art includes many elements, such as game layout charts, storyboards, level layouts, environment illustrations, character designs, model sheets, and GUI designs.
- Each type of concept art fulfills a vital role in the overall game design.
- Sometimes specialized art is required for specific games.
- Each game design is a unique document, so rather than following a strict formula, the design should be adapted to the needs of the game.

This chapter also covered several basic elements of concept art production, including:

- Game layout charts
- Storyboards
- Level layouts
- Environment illustrations
- Character designs
- Model sheets
- Graphical user interface designs

Questions

1. What is a concept artist's role in game development?
2. What is a game design?
3. What are some elements of a game design document?
4. What types of art are generally found in a game design document?
5. What chart is a visual representation of the game showing how the game will be played and all the components of the game?

6. True or false: Because games are not typically linear in nature, storyboards are not used in game development.

7. What type of art is used by concept artists to design a game level?

8. What do level layouts often look like?

9. What can a concept artist do to communicate to a development team the look and mood of an area in a game?

10. True or false: Not all characters in a game need to be designed.

11. What is a sketch of a game character is called?

12. What artwork is used by the development team as a template for creating characters or objects?

13. What is a model sheet?

14. True or false: GUI stands for Graphical User Icon.

15. Do all games have characters?

Answers

1. The person responsible for designing the visual aspects of the game.

2. The document that defines all of the aspects of a game.

3. Detailed descriptions of the characters, settings, story, game play, and technology.

4. Game layout charts, storyboards, level layouts, environment illustrations, character designs, model sheets, and GUI designs.

5. The game layout chart.

6. False.

7. Level layout.

8. Maps.

9. Create an environment illustration.

10. False.

11. A character design.

12. Model sheets.

13. An orthographic, detailed drawing of a character or object used by the development team to create the character or object.

14. False.

15. No.

Discussion Questions

1. Why is art needed in a game design?
2. Why do game design documents need to be unique to the game?
3. Should the game industry standardize game designs?
4. What are some important things to consider when you are designing HUDs?
5. Why is it important to have good game design art?

Exercises

1. Create an outline of a game design document indicating the art needed for each part of the document.
2. Find examples of game concept art in game magazines or on the Internet. Select five of your favorite examples of character design and environment illustrations.
3. Take a game that you own and write down the types of concept art that would be necessary to create a design document for it.

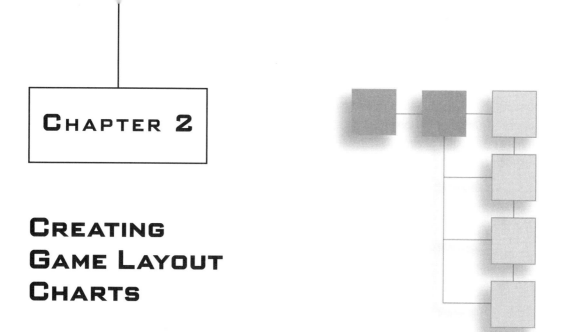

CHAPTER 2

CREATING GAME LAYOUT CHARTS

The game layout chart is the first step in defining the art that you will need for a game design. The chart works as a blueprint of the game, defining how it will work and what it will be. The chart should be a simple-to-follow diagram showing how the game interface will work, the characters or player-controlled elements, the areas or levels, and any other important information relating to the game.

The advantage of creating a game layout chart is that it forces the designer to fully explore how the game will work. Often as a designer and an artist work together on the chart, game elements will change because the designer and artist are getting a better picture of how the game will work. For this reason, it is important to create the chart in such a way that things can be moved around easily.

The game layout chart will help the concept artist determine the art for the design. Each text block in the chart is there to explain a part of the game. As a general rule, a picture of some kind should accompany the text block so there is a visual explanation as well as a written one.

This chapter will explain how to create a game layout chart. It will give you step-by-step instructions along with an explanation of the purpose of each step.

Designing the Style of the Chart

A game layout chart should be designed to convey to the viewer a feeling of what the game will be just by the way it looks. Technically, all the chart has to be is a bunch of text boxes—boxes containing text information—connected by lines or arrows. A simple box and line chart, however, is not very exciting. The game layout chart will be one of the first pieces of art that a reader of the design will encounter. It should express a positive image of the game.

In the example for this book, you will design a fanciful action game for children. The concept of the game is about saving characters from rising floodwaters, so a water motif is appropriate as a background. Figure 2.1 shows a nice watery background for the chart. It works well for a background because it has nice organic gradation of color from the top to the bottom.

Figure 2.1
A water motif is appropriate as a background.

hint

There are many ways to build a game layout chart. You can build the chart by hand by either drawing each text box or using cutouts for each text box, kind of like a scrapbooking project. The most common way to create the chart is by using a computer program. Several programs are useful for building a chart. Many artists use word processors, such as Word or WordPerfect, to build charts because they have great text tools and adequate drawing tools. Vector-drawing programs, such as Illustrator or CorelDRAW, are great tools for creating charts because they have excellent drawing tools and very good text tools. Some programs, such as Visio, are specifically designed for creating charts and have a wide variety of tools for linking text boxes and making charts interactive. The example in this book uses a vector-drawing program to create the chart. However, most other methods of creating charts can easily work with the example.

The fist element to add to the chart is the game title—*Flood*. The word "Flood" is printed across the top of the chart in bold letters, as shown in Figure 2.2.

Figure 2.2
The word "Flood" is printed across the top of the chart in bold letters.

The background motif for the chart is now set. Each page will share this motif to give the chart a consistent look. Most games are too complex for their layout charts to adequately fit on a single page. Tying the chart together with a single motif helps to define each page as part of the chart.

Building the Game Layout Chart

Now that the background for the chart is set, it is time to start building the chart itself.

1. The first step is to design a frame for the text box. A simple box could work, but it does not tell you much about the game. A better choice is to create something that fits with the background motif. A frame of blue bubbles works better as a design element, as shown in Figure 2.3.

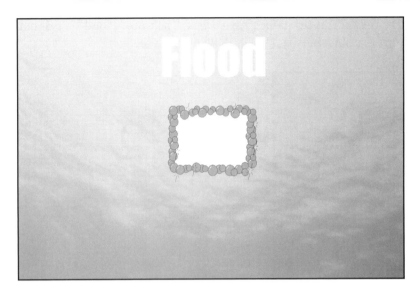

Figure 2.3
A frame of bubbles works well for the design of the text boxes.

2. The very first item on the chart will be a loading screen. A *loading screen* is a graphic that appears at the beginning of a game while the game data is being loaded onto the game system from a CD-ROM or other distribution media. The loading screen is the very first graphic to appear in most games. The graphic can be as simple as the word loading, to as complex as a series of opening screens. One important screen at the beginning of every game is the *legal screen*, which contains legal notifications for the game, such as copyright and trademark information. Figure 2.4 shows the Loading Screen text box.

3. *Flood* is a simple game, so the next screen on the chart is the *title screen*, which introduces the game to the player. Many games will play an introduction video either before or after the title screen. Videos in games are often referred to as FMVs (*Full Motion Videos*). *Flood* does not have an FMV, so only the Title Screen text box is needed for the chart.

4. The next box after the Title Screen box is for the game's *main menu*. This is the central navigation page of the game. It is usually the first menu page in a game, and it connects the player to other menu pages if there are any.

   Arrows connect the text boxes to show the direction of navigation through the game (see Figure 2.5).

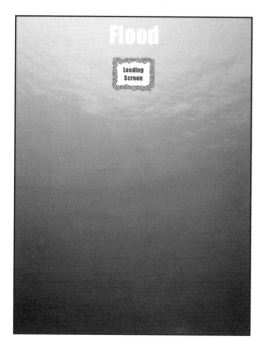

Figure 2.4
The first screen in the game is the loading screen.

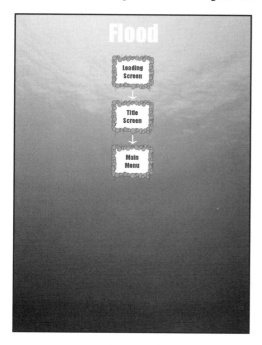

Figure 2.5
Arrows connect the text boxes.

5. The main menu is the hub of the game. From there, the player can start a new game, continue a saved game or change the game options. Up until now, the chart has been linear, with one screen following the next. Now the chart needs to branch out to several screens. Figure 2.6 shows a branching chart. Notice that the arrow to the Game Options box goes in both directions. This indicates that the player will be able to go from the main menu to the game options, and then back to the main menu.

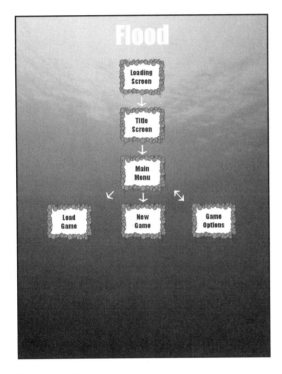

Figure 2.6
Three screens branch off of the main menu screen.

The first box branching from the Main Menu box (on the left side) is the Load Game box. The load game feature allows players to continue playing a game they started earlier. Many games are too time-consuming to play in one sitting. Some games might take days (if not weeks) to complete. Allowing a player to save a game so he can resume it later is a common practice in game design.

In some games, loading a new game will take the player to a new screen; in others, it will just bring up a window. In either case, it is a separate function and should be designated as such in the game layout chart.

The middle text box below the Main Menu box is the New Game box. The new game option allows the player to start a new game. Like the load game option, this option will usually lead to either another screen or a window.

The last text box (on the right side) is the Game Options box. Game options are preferences that the player sets in a game, such as sound levels, graphics quality, animations, and other options. Once preferences are set in the game options screen or window, the player returns to the main menu. Remember, the double-headed arrow indicates that the player can go back and forth from the main menu to the game options.

The next set of text boxes on the chart includes the Play Game box. This box will be expanded on other pages of the chart, but it only occupies one box on this chart. The Play Game box represents the playable part of the game.

To get to the Play Game box, the player either has to load a saved game or create a new game. *Flood* is a character-based game, so the player needs to create a new character to start a new game. In Figure 2.7, notice the placement of the Play Game and Create Character text boxes in the chart. The arrows indicate how the player navigates to the Play Game box.

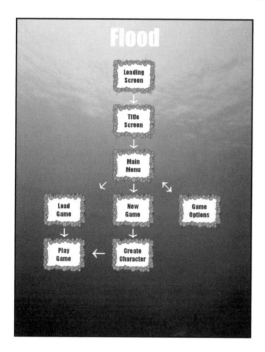

Figure 2.7
The arrows indicate how the player navigates to the Play Game box.

There are only two outcomes of playing the game. Either the player will save and quit the game in progress to resume play later, or the game will end with a win or loss. Figure 2.8 shows the text boxes for these two outcomes.

If the player saves the game, then the game will return to the main menu screen. Figure 2.9 show an arrow going from the Save Game text box to the Main Menu box.

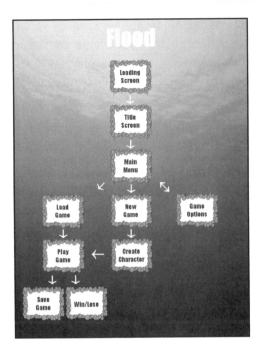

Figure 2.8
The chart shows the outcome of playing the game.

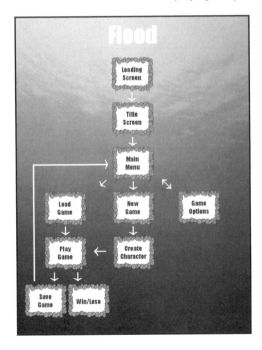

Figure 2.9
The arrow goes from the Save Game box to the Main Menu box.

After the Win/Lose box, the player will also return to the main menu but will go through one more text box on the way. That box is the High Score box. The high score screen in a game shows the player where his score places among that of other players of the game. Figure 2.10 shows the High Score box added, with an arrow going to the Main Menu box.

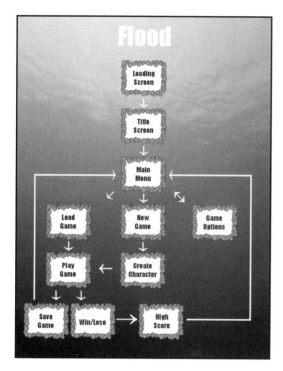

Figure 2.10
The High Score text box is added to the chart.

Now the first page of the chart is almost finished. There is only one more text box that needs to be added, and that is a way for the player to quit the game. The quit game option is usually part of the main menu, so the text box is added so its arrow comes from the Main Menu box, as shown in Figure 2.11.

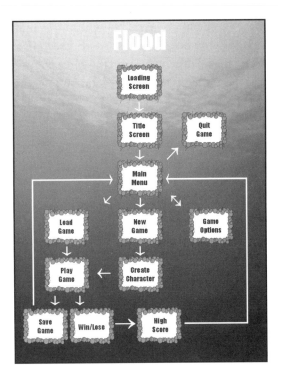

Figure 2.11
The last text box is added to the first page of the chart.

Building the Second Page of the Game Layout Chart

The first page of the game layout chart showed the basic layout of the game navigation, but it did not show the layout of the game levels. The levels are shown on a separate page called the *level layout chart*. The level layout chart is a one-page (or more) diagram of the levels in the game. The chart starts out the same as the first page, with the first text box being Level 1, as shown in Figure 2.12

Flood has a simple game design in which the player takes each level in sequence. The story is about a young dwarf who lives at the bottom of an ancient dwarfish mine. The pumps that keep the lower portion of the mine clear of water have stopped, flooding the young dwarf's homestead. The player has to race against time to reach the upper levels and restart the pumps before the village is completely submerged.

Level 1 is the area around the young dwarf's home. The player must rush to avoid the rising floodwaters. In Level 2, the young dwarf must navigate the lower mines to reach the Level 3 and the dwarfish village. Figure 2.13 shows Levels 2 and 3 added to the chart.

Figure 2.12
The level layout chart starts with Level 1.

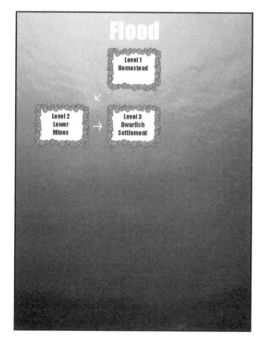

Figure 2.13
Levels 2 and 3 are added to the chart.

Level 3 is where the young dwarf learns about the pumps and the need for a dwarf to reach the surface to restart them. Unfortunately, the only way out is through the central shaft, which is on the other side of where a great dragon lives. The young dwarf must travel through the dragon tunnels to reach the central shaft. Levels 4 and 5 are the dragon tunnels, as shown in Figure 2.14.

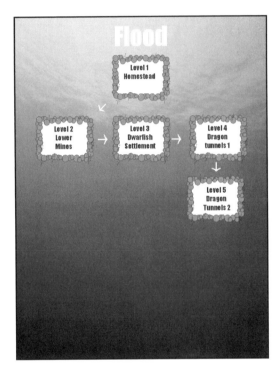

Figure 2.14
Levels 4 and 5 are the dragon tunnels.

After safely navigating the dragon tunnels, the young dwarf must then somehow get past the great dragon in her nest to reach the central shaft. Figure 2.15 shows the next two levels added to the chart.

Once past the central shaft, the young dwarf must find his way through the old abandoned middle mines, which take up Levels 8 and 9 of the game, as shown in Figure 2.16.

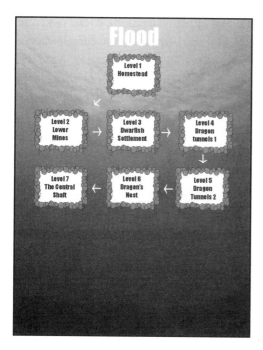

Figure 2.15
The dragon nest and central shaft levels are added to the chart.

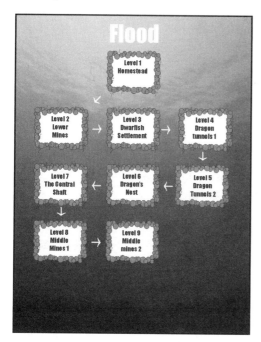

Figure 2.16
The abandoned middle mines take up Levels 8 and 9 of the game.

The middle mines are connected to the upper mines via the machine room. In the machine room, the young dwarf finds that the great pumps were turned off because the dwarves living in the upper mines didn't think there were any other dwarves in the mine. Now the young dwarf must travel through the upper mines to find the leader of the upper dwarves and convince her to turn the pumps back on before the lower dwarves are completely flooded out. Figure 2.17 shows the upper mine levels added to the chart.

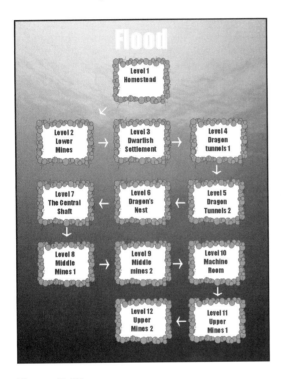

Figure 2.17
The upper mines are added to the chart.

Our young dwarf finally reaches the great pumps in the last level and turns them on, saving the lower dwarves. Figure 2.18 shows the completed level layout chart.

Flood is designed in a linear progression format. Each level is taken in succession, one after the other. In a linear progression game, the player has to complete one level before going to the next. Many story-based games have linear progression formats.

Games designed in a linear progression format give the game designer more control over the game experience. The advantage of a linear progression design is that the designer can orchestrate the game experience, similar to a motion picture production. The downside of this method of game design is that there are no unique user experiences. Every player basically experiences the same thing.

Figure 2.18
The great pumps are the last level of the game.

Other Types of Level Designs

Many games have a more open approach to game design than the linear progression format. In these games, the player has more choices for movement and exploration. The advantage of more choices in game progression is that the player gains a more unique experience. Because different choices lead to different experiences, these games have more replay value. *Replay value* is the measure of a player's desire to replay the game after finishing it the first time. This is an important consideration in game design because most players tend to equate replay value with overall value.

In Figure 2.19, the chart shows a terrain-style open game design. By terrain-style, I mean that you can see each level is connected to all adjacent levels, similar to a terrain map. In many ways, this style of game is really a one-level design broken into smaller sections.

The chart shows Level 1 as the central level in the game. From Level 1, the player can go to Levels 2 through 9, but not Levels 10 through 13. Level 1 has the most available choices, while Levels 10 through 13 have the fewest. In this game, the player can move freely from one level to almost any other level. Each time the player plays the game, the experience can be very different, increasing the replay value of the game.

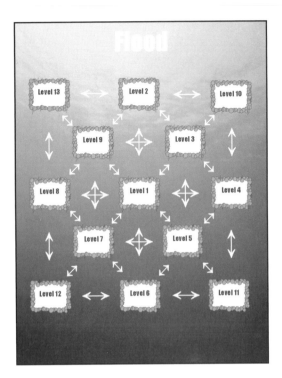

Figure 2.19
Terrain-style open game design

The danger of an open level design, such as the terrain-style approach, is that you have much less control over the player's progress through the game. The player might play through the game and completely bypass some levels. The most interesting part of a game might be in a level that the player never sees because he doesn't happen to go to that level. Variety in a game is an important feature, but it must be balanced with many other important aspects of game design, such as the player's skill progression, story progression, and production resources.

The open terrain-style approach to level design is one extreme, and the linear progression approach is the opposite extreme. By limiting the number of arrows from one level to another, a game designer can create variations on both methods. Figure 2.20 shows how removing some of the arrows changes the completion of the game design.

With the arrows removed, the player has to play through a number of levels to reach Level 13. This approach to level design is called an *open path approach*. The open path approach to game design gives the player some freedom, while still giving the designer some control over the player's progression in the game.

Although the open terrain-style approach to level design seems to give the player the most choices, it still isn't the most open of game designs. The most open approach is one

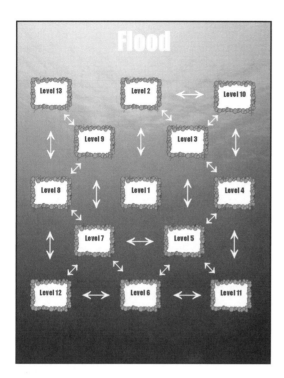

Figure 02.20
Some of the arrows are removed to narrow the player's choices.

in which any level can be accessed from any level. This type of level design is called a *full open approach*. Figure 2.21 shows a chart for a full open level design. Because every level is accessible from every other level, all of the levels are listed without arrows. Arrows are only needed when the paths between levels are limited.

In addition to limiting the path of progression in a game, the designer can also limit access to areas in a game by requiring certain events to take place before a player can progress from one area to another. These events can be almost anything, but the most common event is to have a locked door where the player has to gain access by finding a key or some other device that will open the door. Figure 2.22 shows the open terrain-style game with event blocks in place between some of the levels. The line through the arrow indicates that access to the next level requires some event to take place.

By requiring events to happen before a player can move to the next level, the designer gains more control over the progress of the game. The problem with this method of controlling the player's progress is in how it is implemented. If the event is finding an item, the player might become frustrated if he is not able to locate it. Game designers have to be careful that events are not too difficult or too easy for the player; otherwise, the player might become frustrated with the game and quit playing before he is finished.

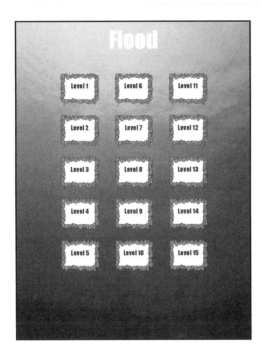

Figure 2.21
The full open level design contains no arrows.

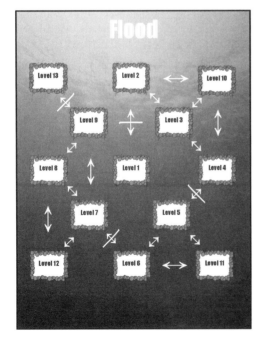

Figure 2.22
Lines through arrows mean that an event has to occur before the player can move to the next level.

Charting Complex Games

As you saw in the previous section, charting levels can sometimes become a complex process. The game artist needs to work closely with the designer to determine the correct way to chart the levels in a game. Some games might have more levels than can be charted on a single page. Other games might have events that change the path of the game during the game. There are no set ways to chart a game. The only general rules are that text boxes are used to explain individual parts of a game, and arrows show progress between the text boxes. Beyond that, the artist can be as creative as necessary to show how the game will be put together. However, the artist must balance clarity with aesthetics to come up with an appropriate chart. A beautiful chart is impractical if it is too cluttered to follow easily. On the other hand, a clearly drawn chart might be boring if there is no design.

Some games might require the artist to create multiple pages of level designs. In these charts, it is often best to have one page that shows how each of the other pages connects. This page becomes a chart of the chart.

Some games might have the path change based on player choices. A good method of dealing with this type of complexity in a chart is to color code the possible paths. Each possibility needs to be charted, but by coloring one path blue while the other is red, you make it easier for the reader to follow the course of the game.

Some games might have the player revisit levels he has already explored. In these games, the level will often change to suit the timing of the player's return. When major changes to a level occur between a player's visits, the level should be treated as a new level. For example, if Level 4 is a village the player first visits before it is destroyed by an earthquake, and then visits again after the earthquake, the level should be designated in the chart as a new level. For the second visit, the level could be designated as Level 4a to indicate that it is based on an earlier level.

Some games might have nonplayable events, such as FMVs or information screens, between levels. These items should be added to the chart between the levels. If the event happens during a level, the event should be placed beside the level, with a line connecting the level to the event to show that the event is part of the level. Figure 2.23 shows an example of an opening FMV attached to the first level of the game.

Figure 2.23
The FMV at the opening of Level 1 is attached with a line.

Summary

The process of charting a game is a combination of game design and art production. In most cases, unless the artist is also the game designer, it is a team effort involving two or more individuals. The job of the concept artist is to design an aesthetically pleasing chart that expresses the feeling of the game while remaining clear and easy to read.

In this chapter, you should have learned the following concepts:

- What a game layout chart is
- How to create backgrounds for game layout charts
- How text boxes are used in game layout charts
- How to chart game elements
- What the different opening game elements are
- What the purpose of the main menu in a game is
- How to chart levels
- How to chart linear progression level layouts
- How to chart terrain-style level layouts

- How to chart open path level layouts
- How to chart full open level layouts
- How to deal with complex level designs

Questions

1. What is a game layout chart?
2. How are game layout charts used?
3. What is the concept artist's role in creating a game layout chart?
4. How is a text box used in a game layout chart?
5. What are some of the opening screens often found in a game?
6. How is a title screen different than a legal screen?
7. What does FMV stand for?
8. What is the hub of the game navigation called?
9. In the game layout chart titled *Flood*, what are the four text boxes attached to the main menu?
10. What does a double-headed arrow indicate on a game layout chart?
11. What are the possible outcomes of playing a game?
12. What is a linear progression level design?
13. Is replay value important in game design?
14. Which is a more open level layout, an open path design or a terrain-style design?
15. Why doesn't a full open design have arrows connecting the levels?

Answers

1. A chart that defines the game and how it works.
2. As a quick reference to explain the game to interested parties.
3. To create the chart under the guidance of the designer.
4. To show unique stages of a game.
5. Loading, legal, and title screens.
6. The legal screen gives legal information, while the title screen gives the game's title.
7. Full Motion Video.
8. Main menu.
9. Load Game, New Game, Game Options, and Quit Game.
10. That the path between the items goes in both directions.

11. Save/quit the game or end the game with a win/loss.

12. A level design in which each successive level must be completed before the player can move on to the next level.

13 Yes.

14. Terrain-style level design.

15. Because the connections between levels are not limited.

Discussion Questions

1. Why is it important for a game layout chart to express the feel of the game?

2. Why is it a good idea to create the game layout chart at the beginning of a game design?

3. How does the game layout chart help the concept artist plan the art for the design?

4. What are the benefits of a game layout chart?

5. What are the advantages and disadvantages of linear versus open level designs?

Exercises

1. Create a game layout chart for your own game design.

2. Create a level layout chart for a terrain-style level design.

3. Create a level layout chart for a game with multiple pages of levels.

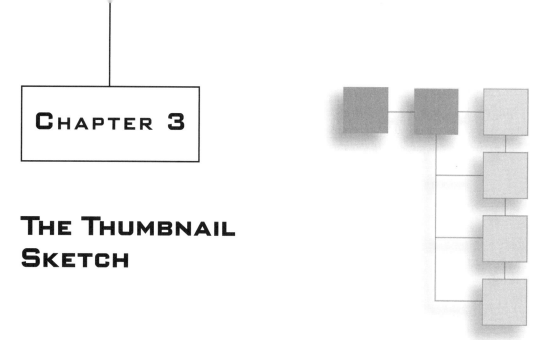

Chapter 3

The Thumbnail Sketch

It is the job of the concept artist to visualize the game. The artist must be able to see the game in his mind, and then communicate his vision in art. The first step in getting the vision on paper is to create small, quick sketches, often called thumbnail sketches. A *thumbnail sketch* is a small drawing no more than three or four inches in any one dimension.

A thumbnail sketch is not a precise drawing; rather, it is a quick, loose sketch of the artist's ideas. It is in these preliminary sketches that the artist begins to work out his ideas of how the game should look. The advantage of doing quick, loose drawings is that the artist can explore multiple ideas without committing significant time to any one idea.

Thumbnail sketches typically are not part of the game design document; rather, they are used to develop the art that will be in the document. The concept artist might be the only person to ever see the thumbnail sketches for a game.

Drawing

Even though a thumbnail sketch isn't part of the design document, and it is rarely seen by anyone other than the concept artist, it still requires good drawing skills for it to be useful. When drawing thumbnail sketches, the artist should work out design issues and develop the look of the game. A skillfully drawn thumbnail sketch will contain more useful information than a sloppy one. Much of this book is about drawing, so a brief discussion of basic drawing techniques is appropriate.

Most people understand a drawing as something created with a pencil and a piece of paper. To really understand drawing, the artist must learn about those two important components.

The Paper

In some ways the paper used in drawing is more important than the instrument used to create the drawing. Figure 3.1 shows a blown-up view of several different paper textures. The texture of the paper can play a big role in how a drawing looks.

Figure 3.1
The paper texture can greatly affect the look of a drawing.

Notice that some of the paper textures in the illustration have very pronounced patterns. Paper is made by pressing organic or synthetic fibers together. The fibers are called *pulp*, and they can come from any number of sources. The fibers are first bleached white, and then pressed together in sheets. The most common source of fiber for paper is wood pulp. Most paper used in art, however, is made from cotton. Cotton paper can be created without leaving any acid residue in the paper, which keeps the paper from changing color and deteriorating.

The texture of the paper can affect the look of the drawing. In Figure 3.2, a pencil stroke is applied to two different paper surfaces. Notice how the pencil lines react differently to the different surfaces.

Figure 3.2
The pencil lines differ depending on the surface texture of the paper.

Paper textures can be used to create drawing effects. If the artist desires a rough, textured drawing, a highly textured paper—such as a cold, pressed watercolor paper—is the best choice. If the artist wants a smoother surface with less texture, a hot press paper is a good choice.

Another important aspect of the paper is its tooth. *Tooth* is the term artists use to describe the abrasive quality of a drawing surface. The higher the abrasive quality, the more pigment is transferred from the pencil to the paper. The paper's tooth is a combination of the texture and softness of the paper. The smoother the texture and the softer the paper, the less likely it will be to pick up much pigment. The rougher the texture and the harder the fibers, the more likely the paper will pick up more pigment. A paper that picks up a lot of pigment is said to have a lot of tooth. A paper that picks up little pigment is said to have little or no tooth.

The Pencil

The other half of the drawing equation is the pencil or drawing instrument. There are a number of drawing pencils on the market. Most are adequate, but there are a few things to understand about the type of pencil the artist uses to draw and sketch. Pencils use a substance called *graphite* that is applied to the paper to create a drawing. Graphite can come in many variations of hardness. The harder the graphite, the less likely it will be transferred to the paper in the drawing process. Soft graphite will transfer much easier than hard graphite. Figure 3.3 shows the differences between pencils with different graphite hardnesses. The harder graphite is on the left, and the softer graphite is on the right. Notice that the pencil marks on the right are much darker than the ones on the left.

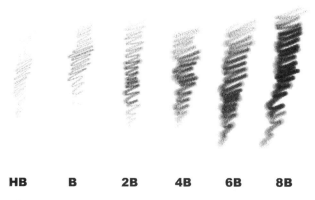

HB   B   2B   4B   6B   8B

Figure 3.3
Softer graphite pencils transfer easier to the paper.

In addition to the hardness of the graphite, another important aspect of a drawing pencil is the purity of the graphite. Some cheaper pencils will have impurities in the graphite that will cause the pencil to scratch the drawing surface when the artist uses them. These small impurities can cause problems when the artist tries to draw because not only do the impurities scratch the surface, they also keep the graphite from transferring. It is usually a good idea to test a few pencils to check for impurities before you settle on the ones you want to use in your drawings.

Drawing Technique

There are almost as many ways to draw as there are artists, so this section of the book will not cover all of them. The most important aspects of drawing thumbnail sketches are speed and clarity. The object here is not to produce a finished drawing; rather, it is to quickly express and save an idea for later development.

Drawing styles range from tight to loose. A *tight drawing* is very precise, with every line or gradation in the drawing. A *loose drawing* is imprecise and more abstract in nature.

A precise drawing is usually called a rendering. *Renderings* are drawings used to define the elements being drawn in great detail. When rendering, most artists will use *reference*, which is an artistic term used to designate the source material an artist refers to when he creates a work of art. Reference can be anything the artist looks at while working on the art. Photographs are the most common form of reference, but many artists prefer to look at the actual objects they are trying to depict. Because renderings take time to create, they are usually not used as thumbnail sketches. Figure 3.4 is a rendering of a person. In this picture, great care was taken to be as precise as possible, right down to the eyelashes.

Figure 3.4
A rendering is a precise drawing.

Thumbnail sketches tend to be loose because the artist is drawing an idea and often does not have a reference to look at while drawing. Thumbnail sketches do not contain great detail for the same reason. Figures 3.5 and 3.6 are loose drawings more typical of a thumbnail sketch.

These sketches were obviously created quickly, with only minimal thought given to the fine detail of the subject matter.

Figure 3.5
Thumbnail sketches are generally loose drawings.

Figure 3.6
Often in a thumbnail sketch, detail is merely suggested.

Pencil Strokes

Drawings are made up of pencil strokes, which can be bold, light, flowing, or smooth. They affect both the look and feeling of a drawing. The type of pencil strokes an artist uses to create a drawing is a personal choice and is as individual as a person's handwriting. Beginning artists should explore different ways of drawing until they are comfortable with a drawing technique.

Figure 3.7 shows a simple zigzag stroke. This stroke is one of the quickest ways to shade in an area. The drawback of a stroke like this is that although it tends to work well for shading flat areas, it does not express much about the nature of the surface being shaded.

Figure 3.7
A zigzag stroke is one of the quickest ways to shade an area.

Figure 3.8 shows a stroke that is similar to the zigzag stroke, but is created with more of a scrubbing motion. This stroke is used for fine, smooth gradations in drawings. It is not an expressive stroke; rather, it is a stroke used for smooth shading. When using this kind of stroke, the artist is attempting to hide any evidence of the individual pencil strokes.

Figure 3.8
A scrubbing motion can create a smooth gradation.

Figure 3.9 shows a directional stroke. Each stroke is a separate line drawn with the pencil. Directional strokes can be used for shading, just like zigzag strokes, but they can be more expressive because they can follow the direction of the shape.

Figure 3.9
Directional strokes are separate lines drawn next to each other.

A variation on the directional stroke is a weighted directional stroke. In it, the artist applies more pressure to one end of the stroke than the other. Figure 3.10 shows a weighted directional stroke used to draw a lock of hair.

Figure 3.10
A lock of hair can be drawn using a weighted directional stroke.

By crossing the direction of the pencil strokes, the artist can create a new shading method called *crosshatching*. Figure 3.11 shows some stone brick rendered with a crosshatch stroke.

Figure 3.11
Crosshatching is another method of pencil shading.

Sometimes the artist can use pencil strokes to describe an object. In Figure 3.12, pencil strokes are used to create a pine tree, a branch of leaves, and some grass around a rock.

These are just a few types of strokes that an artist can use in drawing. There are as many variations as an artist can imagine.

Figure 3.12
Pencil strokes can be used to describe an object.

Creating the Thumbnail Sketch

As stated earlier, thumbnail sketches are quick idea drawings used by artists to develop several ideas while working out a larger or more detailed drawing. Following is a step-by-step approach to a quick thumbnail sketch. The subject is a subway station. In Figure 3.13, the subway station is quickly roughed out in very light strokes of the pencil. By using very light strokes, the artist is able to explore the drawing without becoming committed to any single line. In this way, changes can be made without the artist worrying about erasing lines.

Notice that the light outlines contain multiple lines and look somewhat sloppy. During the early stages of a thumbnail sketch, the artist should not worry about being too precise with the drawing.

Figure 3.13
Light construction lines are used at the beginning of the drawing.

In the next stage of the drawing, a straight edge is used to lay out the more mechanical areas of the station. The use of a straight edge for mechanical lines can speed up the drawing process and give the artist more control over the drawing. Curves can also be used as a guide for the artist, but they are more often used in more detailed rendering. The idea here is to lay out a scene as quickly as possible. Figure 3.14 shows the subway station with most of the basic lines drawn in.

Notice that some of the heavier lines do not follow the original layout. That was why the original layout was drawn in lightly.

Now you can populate the subway station with passengers and a few advertisements, as shown in Figure 3.15.

This is about all you need in a thumbnail sketch. This drawing took only a few minutes to create, and even though it is rough, the artist can get a good idea of how the scene will look from this angle.

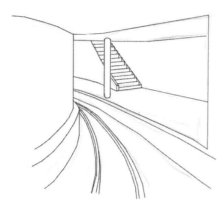

Figure 3.14
Heavier lines are used to better define the subway station.

Figure 3.15
Thumbnail sketches are not detailed sketches, so the people and ads are drawn very loosely.

In Figure 3.16, the artist is trying to work out an angle of view for a scene where a soldier is hiding from a mech. There are three different angles of view. The quick thumbnail sketches, while not very refined, still give the artist ample information for investigating different angles.

Each of the thumbnail sketches in Figure 3.16 has a different dynamic feel. The upper-left sketch is somewhat static, with very little tension between the foreground character and the background mech. In the middle and right sketches, the character's pose is more animated, adding to the drama of the scene. In both of these drawings, the mech is closer and drawn from an angle that makes it more menacing. No matter how much detail is added to the first drawing, it will never have the drama and tension of the other two drawings.

Figure 3.16
The three thumbnail sketches show multiple angles of a soldier and a mech.

Character Thumbnails

One of the biggest uses of thumbnail sketches is for exploring ideas for characters. Characters are the focal point of a game. Having interesting characters can make a big impact on how players perceive the game. The first step in creating a good game character is to work out the ideas in thumbnail form.

The nice thing about thumbnail sketching of characters is that the artist can follow his imagination. The sketches are first drawn loosely as the artist searches for an idea, and then they are refined enough to give the artist a clear picture of the major features of the character. Figure 3.17 is a thumbnail of a cartoon character. The character is much shorter and wider than a normal human.

One way to design a unique character is to exaggerate the character's features. In Figure 3.17, the woman's face is very wide with a large nose and glasses that are so powerful that her eyes appear to be twice their normal size.

Another imaginative approach to designing a character is to blend features of different animals or humans. Figure 3.18 is a creature design that borrows features from several different animals. Notice the very light construction lines in the picture.

Figure 3.17
A thumbnail sketch of a cartoon character

Figure 3.18
Features from several animals were used to create this creature.

Sometimes it is useful to put the character in a setting to help the artist see him or her in context. A setting will help to define the character and give it scale. The earlier sketches were of a character alone. Figure 3.19 shows a character by a tree. The tree and the owl on the tree branch help to define the character as a person who lives in the forest. The spear further defines the character as a warrior.

One trick that is useful in doing thumbnail sketches is to copy the original sketch to experiment with different options. In Figure 3.20, the fairy is copied on the paper twice. In the first copy, butterfly wings are added. In the second copy, bee wings are added. This saves the artist time because the fairy does not have to be redrawn, and the artist can experiment with multiple wing types to find the one that works best for the game.

Figure 3.19
Sometimes a character will be drawn into a setting.

Figure 3.20
Different wings are drawn onto the copies of the fairy.

Design Tool

Many artists will want to jump right in and draw a finished drawing right away. The problem with going directly to the finished drawing is that there is no plan, and the drawing will suffer because not enough thought was put into the design. It is a much better idea to work out the overall design in a thumbnail sketch. Even just a few quick sketches will help the artist define and plan a good design for a final drawing. Figure 3.21 is a quick sketch of a jungle scene with a safari guy in the foreground. The shapes are roughed in quickly with bold strokes to show where the light and dark areas will be.

Figure 3.21
Sometimes a character will be drawn into a setting.

It is easy to change the design of the drawing at the thumbnail level because the drawings are quick and the artist hasn't made a big time or effort commitment. If the design doesn't look good in the thumbnail sketch, chances are it will not look good in the finished drawing either. The more design elements that an artist can work out in loose thumbnail sketches, the better the finished drawing's design will be.

Summary

This chapter covered the basics of drawing and creating thumbnail sketches. In this chapter, you should have learned the following concepts:

- Sketching ideas is the first step in creating concept art for games.
- A thumbnail sketch is a fast and easy way to put an artist's ideas on paper.
- Different papers have different textures and react differently to the pencil.
- Pencils range in hardness.
- Different types of pencil strokes are used in drawing.
- There are several steps in creating a thumbnail sketch.
- Creating multiple views of a scene in thumbnail sketches can lead to more dynamic designs.
- Thumbnail sketches are used to design characters.
- Thumbnails sketches are used to design a drawing before the artist starts the final version.

Questions

1. What is another name for a quick idea sketch?

2. True or false: Artists should take a long time to create a thumbnail sketch.

3. What does a paper's tooth refer to?

4. Which paper will pick up more pigment from a drawing instrument—a paper with a lot of tooth or a paper with little tooth?

5. Is an 8B pencil softer than a 2B pencil?

6. What is the difference between a tight and a loose drawing?

7. Why are thumbnail drawings usually loose drawings?

8. Are thumbnail drawings considered rendering?

9. Should all artists use the same type of pencil strokes when creating a thumbnail sketch?

10. What is a zigzag stroke?

11. When are light pencil lines used to create a thumbnail sketch?

12. True or false: Usually the first sketch is the best, so an artist rarely needs to do more than one or two thumbnail sketches.

13. Are thumbnails sketches used much in character designs?

14. How can copying a thumbnail sketch help an artist experiment with a character design?

15. Should an artist use thumbnail sketches to plan the design of a picture?

Answers

1. A thumbnail sketch.

2. False.

3. The abrasive qualities of the paper.

4. A paper with a lot of tooth.

5. Yes.

6. Tight drawings are precise drawings, while loose drawings are not.

7. They are created quickly and usually without reference.

8. Usually they are not renderings.

9. No. Pencil strokes are unique to the artist's style of drawing.

10. A pencil stroke made with a back-and-forth motion without taking the pencil from the paper.

11. At the very beginning of the drawing.

12. False.

13. Yes.

14. The artist can experiment with detail without having to redraw the drawing.

15. Yes.

Discussion Questions

1. How does the paper affect a drawing?

2. How does the softness of the graphite in a pencil affect the drawing?

3. Why shouldn't an artist spend a lot of time working on a thumbnail sketch?

4. Should an artist put a lot of detail in a thumbnail drawing?

5. Why should an artist plan a drawing by doing a few thumbnail sketches first?

Exercises

1. Do several thumbnail sketches of a game scene. Try to vary the tension and drama of each sketch.

2. Create several thumbnail sketches of a wizard for a game. Try different clothing and genders as well as different creatures to find the best design.

3. Plan a major drawing by using thumbnail sketches to design the major parts of it. Try multiple view angles.

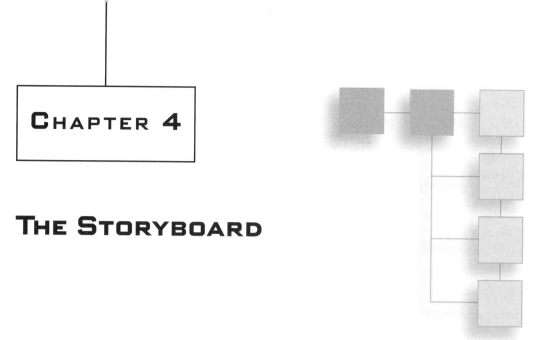

CHAPTER 4

THE STORYBOARD

Storyboarding has proven to be one of the most effective ways to plan a video game. There are many reasons to use storyboards in games. The following list highlights just a few of them:

- Storyboarding saves time and money.
- Storyboarding helps show sequences that are difficult to explain.
- Storyboarding helps to communicate the game concept to all involved in development.
- Storyboarding helps the design team work out difficult game problems.

Creating Games Takes Time and Money

Creating video games takes a lot of money and effort. It is expensive to create 3D models for game characters and worlds. The cost gets even higher with programming and animation. Trying to create a game without a plan can result in wasted time and money. Storyboarding helps the design team to plan the production. By visualizing the game in storyboard format, the design team can communicate to the development team a consistent vision of the game, reducing the potential for wasted effort.

Games are getting more and more complex. Production budgets are getting higher, and development teams are getting larger. In many instances the development team might be located in separate facilities, sometimes on opposite ends of the planet. All of these factors point to the need for efficient and effective communication. Because a storyboard is a method of communication, it helps development companies keep their productions on track.

Often games have very specific release dates. If a game gets bogged down in development, the financial impact on the publisher can be enormous. It is always wiser to spend a little more time creating a clear picture of the game in the planning stages than it is to plunge

55

into development and get stalled midway through the process because one or more team members did not get a clear picture of the project.

Games Can Be Difficult to Explain

A written description of a game is not enough. Many concepts or sequences in a video game are difficult to communicate with just a written document. The old adage that a picture is worth a thousand words is particularly true in video game development. For example, if the game designer wants a particular antagonist to attack the player in a certain way, it will be much easier for him to show that attack in a sequence of drawings than to use lengthy descriptions.

The storyboard helps simplify the communication process in game design. Although a video game might have sound and player interaction, it is still very much a visual medium. The whole premise of video games is that the player interacts with what he sees on the screen. It makes perfect sense that visual media, such as storyboards, are used when you are designing for a visual medium, such as a game.

Storyboarding Helps with Communication

Beyond the team that actually puts the game together, there are many people involved in the development and marketing of a video game. These people might include producers, product managers, executives, investors, analysts, stockholders, members of the press, and many others. Most of these people want to see the game as soon as possible. The storyboard is their first glimpse of what the game will look like. The storyboard is a window into the future through which everyone can begin to see the possibilities of the game.

The bigger the game project, the more important it is to show early on how the game will look and play. This is particularly important for those who have invested in the project. They want to see that their money is going to a great product. This puts a lot of pressure on the storyboard artist, who must create storyboards that convey an accurate picture of the game. Any failure on the part of the storyboard artist to give an accurate picture of the game could result in a very good game idea getting canceled because the investors are not able to catch the vision of the game from the art.

As I stated earlier, there are many interested parties in a video game project. One of those is the press. Many video game magazines carry early art from games. Sometimes the art in these publications includes storyboards from a highly anticipated game. This makes it doubly important for the artist to create great storyboards because the art might appear in a national magazine.

Storyboarding Aids in Problem Solving

The last, yet most practical, reason to use storyboards in game development is to help the design team work out difficult problems. Using storyboards of possible solutions, the design team can find a solution that not only works in concept but also works visually. Sometimes the simple act of drawing a number of solutions will spark even better ideas for a solution.

With the increased complexity of games, difficult problems often arise. For example, a fighting game might require each character to have a special attack. Because every attack must have a corresponding defense and each character has a different fighting style, the problem becomes very difficult. Through storyboarding each attack and how each character in the game defends the attack, the problem becomes more manageable.

What Are Storyboards Used for in Games?

Storyboards are used for a number of purposes in the process of game development. Following is a list of some of the most common areas in which storyboards are used to create games:

- Planning cinematic sequences
- Developing animation
- Showing complex action
- Showing non-player actions

Cinematic Sequences

Many games use cinematic sequences during the game to explain story elements or introduce characters to the player. A *cinematic sequence* is a non-interactive movie. It generally is used to give the player information to help him play the game.

In the early days of video games, players were presented with text from which they could read important game information. This was because most early systems did not have the power to display video. Some games would use a series of still images to help the player through the story. In the last several years, game systems have become powerful enough to display cinematic sequences. Now most games use video clips to explain the game to the player.

Storyboarding for cinematic sequences is similar to storyboarding for movies. The concept artist uses the storyboards to direct the action and camera movement from scene to scene throughout the sequence. The storyboards are then given to the development group responsible for creating the sequence.

Most cinematic sequences in video games are created as 3D animations. Some games, however, might call for live action or 2D animation. The storyboard is the foundation of any animated sequence. Although storyboards are frequently used in live-action shoots, they are not as critical as they are in animation. In a live-action shoot, often the director will take advantage of the set and cast to improve a sequence. With animation, the process is very different.

When animating, the storyboard is the base from which each animation sequence is developed. The animators take the storyboards and create layouts from them that are highly detailed versions of each action in a sequence. If the animation is 2D, the layouts are used to create the individual frames of animation. In 3D animation, the layouts are used to create the characters and settings, and then the storyboards are used to set up the rendering of the animation. This is similar to a live-action shoot, with the exception that the animation is more planned than in a live-action shoot.

Animation

Character-based games have many animation sequences for the characters. One character might have more than one hundred animation sequences. Not only is it sometimes difficult to keep track of all these animation sequences, it is also difficult to show the animators on the team how a character is going to move in a game. Storyboards are often used to show animation sequences for a character so the animator is able to see how the action is designed to happen.

Animators will often sketch out their animation sequences prior to animating the characters in a game. By sketching the character movement and working out the details on paper first, the artist saves time and money. The game designer and other production managers can review the storyboarded animation sequence to verify that it is consistent with the other animation in the game.

Complexity

Games are becoming more complex as systems get more powerful and players become more sophisticated. Often the game designer is faced with a particularly difficult area of a game. There might be several factors that will change the outcome of a given event in that area. For example, the player might enter a crowded room looking for a clue to a mystery. The player can talk to several other characters in the room, and the outcome of the event might change based on whom the player talks to and what he talks about. Storyboarding the event is a complex task in itself, but not as complex as building it in the game. By carefully storyboarding the event, the designer can better explore the potential options, but also define them so the development team can accurately create the event.

Other complex elements in a game might have nothing at all to do with the actual game play. These elements include character creation, game setup, and game editors. The concept artist will likely be called upon to create these game elements in storyboard form to help define exactly how they will work in the game.

Non-Player Actions

Many games will have a significant number of non-player characters. A *non-player character* is any character in a game not controlled directly by the player. The game's artificial intelligence (or AI, as it is often called in the industry) controls all these characters. *Artificial intelligence* is the software that tells the game how to react to the player's actions. Storyboards are often used to show what the non-player characters do in a game. In a fighting game, for example, the player might fight a number of opponents, all with very specific fighting styles. These fighting styles are first visualized in the storyboards.

Are Storyboards Important?

Storyboards definitely play an important role in game design and development. They are the first visualization of sequential action in a game. As games become larger and more complex, storyboards will continue to be valuable tools for the design team to communicate with all those involved in the production of the game.

Now that you have examined the importance of storyboarding in game design, it is time to learn how storyboards are made.

Learning about Storyboards

A storyboard is a single panel with a picture and a description. Figure 4.1 shows a blank storyboard. There are two large blank areas and other smaller blank areas. Each of these areas has a purpose.

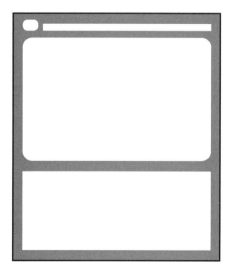

Figure 4.1
Each area on a storyboard has a purpose.

The upper, larger blank area of a storyboard is the *picture area*. This is where the concept artist draws a picture that depicts the action that the storyboard is supposed to represent. It usually has rounded corners to represent the rounded corners on a TV screen. The other large blank area just below the picture area is the description area. It is here that a written description of the screen is placed. It is also here that any specific directions are given.

In the upper-left corner there is a small box with rounded corners. See Figure 4.2 for a close-up view of the box. This box is used to indicate the number of the frame; it is often called the *frame number box*. Because storyboards show a sequence of actions, there are usually at least two (and often several more) individual panels in a series of storyboards. The series and panel number are placed in the frame number box. In Figure 4.2, the panel is the third in the forty-second storyboard sequence.

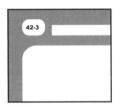

Figure 4.2
The series and panel number are placed in the frame number box.

The long horizontal box next to the frame number box is used to indicate where the storyboard fits in the game. It is called the *scene box*. Here the artist indicates the exact location in the game of the storyboarded sequence. In Figure 4.3, the sequence is in the control room of Level 7.

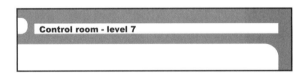

Figure 4.3
The scene box is where the artist writes the location of the storyboard.

Although it is simple, the layout of the storyboard panel is important. The numbers in the upper-left corner make it easy for the team to locate any sequence. The scene box helps them to understand where the storyboard is located in the design.

This example of a storyboard panel is only one of many variations. Figure 4.4 shows another example of a storyboard panel. This panel is designed for digital development so that the entire panel can fit on a computer screen.

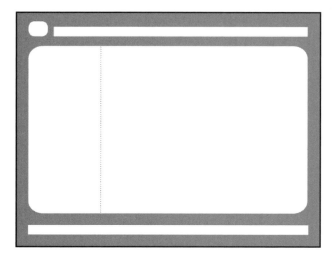

Figure 4.4
This storyboard panel is designed so it fits on a computer screen.

The panel has only one major area, which is divided into two sections separated by a dashed line. The scene description and directions are printed to the left of the line, and the picture is drawn to the right of the line.

Camera Direction

When developing storyboard panels, the concept artist needs to understand basic camera directions. *Camera directions* are drawn directions that appear on a storyboard to tell the animator or director what the camera will be doing during a scene. For most storyboards in games, camera directions are not important because the player and the game code control the camera. The cinematic sequences require camera direction, the same as storyboards for motion pictures.

The most common camera direction is the *zoom* or *truck action*. Most people are acquainted with a zoom lens on a camera. The zoom feature of the lens allows the photographer to change how close an object or character looks in a picture. The word "truck" comes from the motion picture industry, where they sometimes mount cameras on small trolleys on tracks. By moving the camera along the track, the camera can move in or away from a scene. In either case, the basic camera direction is to move from a wider shot into a close-up shot. Figure 4.5 shows the storyboard direction for the zoom or truck camera action.

The edges of the picture panel represent the wide shot. The inner box represents the close-up at the end of the zoom or truck camera direction. The arrows show the direction of the zoom. If the arrows are reversed, then the camera direction is reversed, and the beginning shot is the close-up and the end shot is the wide shot, as shown in Figure 4.6.

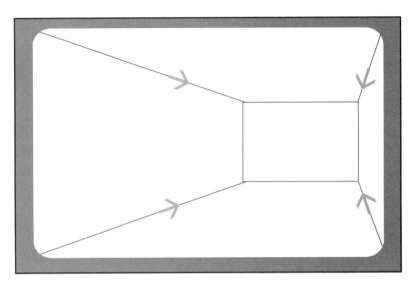

Figure 4.5
The inside box represents the end of the zoom or truck camera direction.

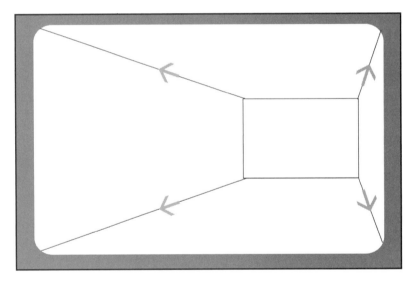

Figure 4.6
Reversing the arrows also reverses the camera direction.

Another important camera direction is pan. *Pan* means to move the camera parallel to the scene. Cameras can pan in any direction. Figure 4.7 shows the storyboard directions for a pan camera action.

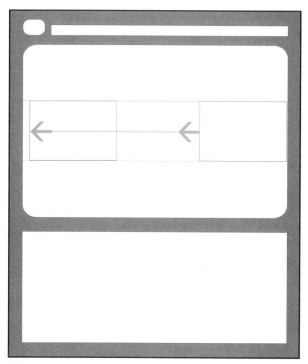

Figure 4.7
Pan is another basic camera direction.

The small box on the right is the start camera view, and the two lines on the left of the box are the track of the camera as it passes over the scene. The arrows indicate the direction of the pan camera action. The small box on the left is the end camera view.

Sometimes the camera direction will call for more than one move within a single scene. The artist can draw a new storyboard or put more than one camera direction on a single storyboard. In Figure 4.8, the camera zooms in from an establishing shot and then pans from right to left across the scene.

There can be any variation on the simple camera directions of zoom and pan; it is up to the imagination of the artist. A variation that often happens is a combination of a zoom and a pan, as shown in Figure 4.9. The camera pulls back a little as it pans across the scene.

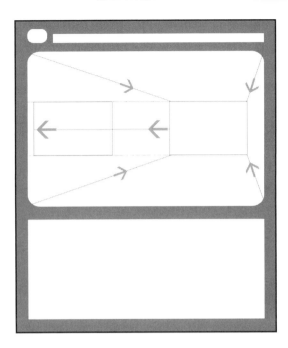

Figure 4.8
Sometimes more than one camera direction is given in a single storyboard panel.

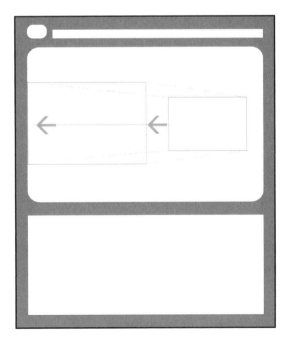

Figure 4.9
The camera pulls back as it pans across the scene.

Written Directions

In addition to drawn directions, the concept artist might want to write additional directions below the picture on the panel. The additional directions help make the storyboard as clear as possible to the viewer. For example, in Figure 4.9, the camera is moving from right to left and pulling back at the same time. The artist might want the two movements to start at different times. Offsetting movement times often will add drama to a scene. In the camera directions, the artist might write the following:

> Start pan from right to left, and then begin pull back after the pan is about one quarter across the scene.

Typically, exact frame timing is not included in the storyboards, but sometimes when the concept artist is also an animator, this information will be included. Usually the animation director adds the timing in the animation layout phase. If the concept artist understood timing and wanted to add some timing notes in the storyboards, the written directions would look like this:

> Hold on scene from Frame 0 to Frame 60, and then ease into 120-frame pan. Begin truck out at Frame 90. Ease out of both pan and truck at Frame 180 and hold for 60 frames.

The terms *ease-in* and *ease-out* are used to indicate the gradual increase and decrease in camera speed, respectively. Ease-in will reduce the feeling of being jerked into the camera movement. The ease-out directions help to eliminate jarring stops to the camera movement.

Special-Use Panels

Sometimes a scene will call for a special use panel because of the size of the scene. For example, a scene might be very wide, with the camera panning over an extended portion. Trying to draw the scene in the standard panel would be difficult, so special-use panels are available for this purpose. Figure 4.10 shows a special-use panel for extra-wide scenes.

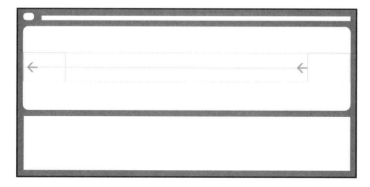

Figure 4.10
Wide scenes use a wide storyboard panel.

Some scenes might be more vertical in nature. Rather than using a wide panel for these scenes, long panels are available, as shown in Figure 4.11.

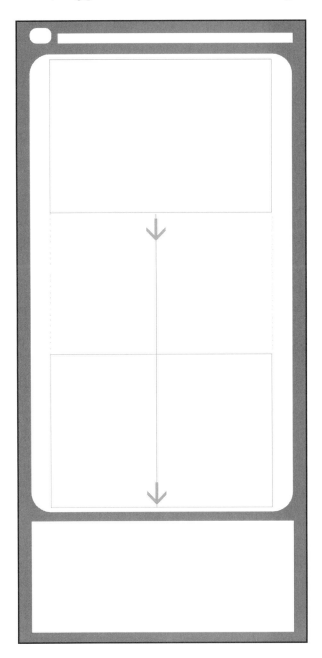

Figure 4.11
Vertical panels are also available.

In situations in which the scene is very complex, the concept artist might want to have a larger drawing area. These special-use panels are also available. Figure 4.12 shows an example of a larger drawing-area panel.

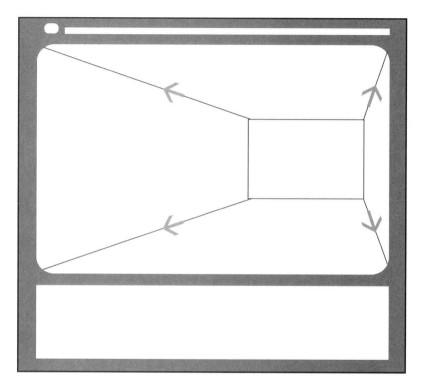

Figure 4.12
The artist can also choose a larger panel for complex scenes.

In addition to these variations, the artist can always create panels to suit the needs of the project. This book's CD includes some printable samples of the panels shown in this chapter.

Showing Action

Storyboards are used to show sequences of action. The action might be something a character does in the game, or it might show an interface sequence for game navigation. Central to this theme, the artist must break down the action into individual panels. Figure 4.13 shows how a scene was broken down for a short sequence showing the ninja shooting an arrow at a target. The three main parts of the scene are the ninja shooting, the arrow in flight, and the arrow striking the target.

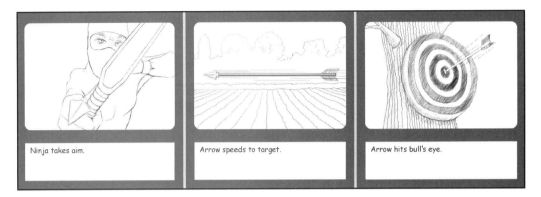

| Ninja takes aim. | Arrow speeds to target. | Arrow hits bull's eye. |

Figure 04.13
The artist breaks down the action in a storyboard.

Each action is unique. If the artist left out one of the storyboard panels, the scene would change dramatically. On the other hand, an extra panel of the ninja drawing the bow would not add significantly to the scene.

Breaking down a scene is an art form in itself. The artist needs to visualize the sequence of events, and then divide them into their separate parts. Thumbnails are a great way to get each part of the sequence down on paper. After all the parts are visualized in at least a rough sketch form, the artist then needs to work out the views of the action. If the storyboard is for a cinematic sequence, the artist will be free to design camera angles and camera directions. If the sequence is part of the game, the artist needs to visualize the player's view of the events.

It is important to remember that the object of the storyboard is to communicate to the development team the ideas of the game design. Creativity is good, but communication must take precedence over other concerns. The artist must plan the panels so that all the important information is given and none is left out.

Summary

This chapter covered many aspects of storyboard development. In this chapter, you should have learned the following concepts:

- Why storyboards are used in game development
- What storyboards are used for in game development
- The basic layout of a storyboard panel and its purposes
- Basic camera directions for storyboards

- Special-use panels and their purposes
- Breaking down action in a storyboard

You should now understand the basic parts and purposes of the storyboard panel. You should also understand how to execute simple camera directions and break down action for a set of storyboards.

Questions

1. If storyboarding each part of a game takes work, how does it save the development company money?
2. Why are storyboards used now more than in the past in game development?
3. How do storyboards help simplify the communication process of complex sequences?
4. What are often the first visual images of the game design shown to the development and marketing teams?
5. How are storyboards used to solve complex problems in a design?
6. What type of storyboards in games are very similar to those in motion pictures?
7. What is the base from which each animation sequence is created?
8. Why is a storyboard for animation more important than one for live action?
9. Why are storyboards used to show character animation?
10. What is the frame number box used for in a storyboard panel?
11. What is the scene box used for?
12. How does the artist indicate a camera movement from a wide shot to a close-up shot?
13. What direction is used for moving the camera from one side of a scene to another, parallel to the scene?
14. What purpose is a long, horizontal storyboard panel used for?
15. Why does a concept artist need to break down a sequence into individual actions?

Answers

1. Mistakes in development will often cost much more than creating storyboards.
2. Games are increasing in complexity.
3. They give a picture of the events so viewers can quickly understand them.
4. Storyboards.
5. By showing multiple solutions.
6. Those used to design cinematic sequences.

7. Storyboards.

8. The director of a live-action sequence has more creative freedom in using the set and cast.

9. To help animators understand the animations needed for each character.

10. To indicate the panel number and the set number.

11. To show the location of the set of panels within a game.

12. By using the zoom or truck camera direction.

13. The pan camera direction.

14. To storyboard wide scenes.

15. To show the complete sequence so nothing is left out.

Discussion Questions

1. Why is it important to use storyboards in game development?

2. What ways can storyboards be used in game development?

3. How can storyboarding save money?

4. How can storyboards help solve difficult problems?

5. Why is it important to use storyboards in developing animation?

Exercises

1. Use a series of storyboards to show how a character might jump over an obstacle.

2. Create an opening cinematic for a game using a series of storyboards. Use at least two major camera movements.

3. Create a storyboard for an extra-wide scene. Indicate the camera movement over the panel.

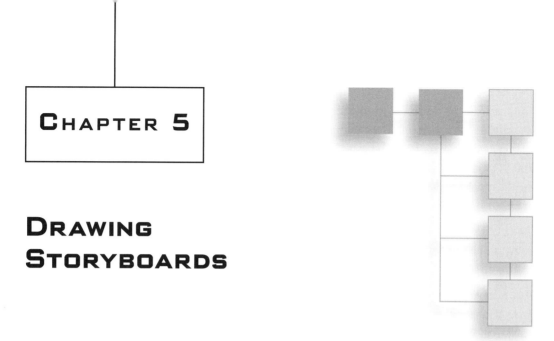

CHAPTER 5

DRAWING STORYBOARDS

Drawing good storyboards is a demanding task. The drawings must be simple and clear. The artist must have good drawing skills and understand perspective, design, motion, volume, shading, and figure drawing, some of which will be covered in this chapter. Each of these skills is important for the artist to develop simple yet clear drawings.

Drawing a good storyboard takes more than just good drawing skills. The artist must also understand the purpose for the storyboards. Storyboards are a communication medium, and like any other communication media, the storyboard must fill its role. Storyboards communicate through pictures. The pictures need to show those looking at the game design a clear image of what the game will look like. For example, a nice picture of a character in a corridor from an extreme angle might look great, but will the character ever be seen from that angle in the game? If not, then the picture is not fulfilling its role in the design.

This chapter will show you how to draw good storyboards. It will briefly cover basic drawing skills. It will also give you a step-by-step look at the development of a series of storyboards.

Basic Drawing Skills

Even though storyboards are primarily for communication, they are still art, and therefore good artistic skills are necessary. The next section will cover basic drawing skills to help you improve your ability to draw good storyboards. The skills that will be covered include:

- Perspective
- Composition
- Shading

Perspective

Perspective is the representation of objects or characters in a picture so they appear to relate spatially as they would to the eye in nature. In the natural world, items appear smaller the farther away they are from the viewer. For example, if someone is standing next to the viewer, that person will appear large. If that person were to walk away from the viewer, he or she would appear to decrease in size. When an artist draws a scene, objects and characters need to be sized so they are correct in relation to other objects or characters in a scene.

One of the most common ways for an artist to correctly establish the sizes of objects in a scene is to use linear perspective. *Linear perspective* is the process of using lines drawn from a vanishing point on the horizon to correctly size the objects or characters in a drawing.

To understand how perspective works, you need to understand the concept of a horizon line. A *horizon line* is formed where the ground meets the sky. In Figure 5.1, the darker gray area on the bottom represents the ground, and the lighter gray on the top represents the sky. The black line where the two meet is the horizon line.

Figure 5.1
The horizon line is between the ground and the sky.

The horizon line forms the basis for linear perspective. It changes depending on the angle used in the picture. For example, viewing a plane in the air will lower the horizon line, as shown in Figure 5.2.

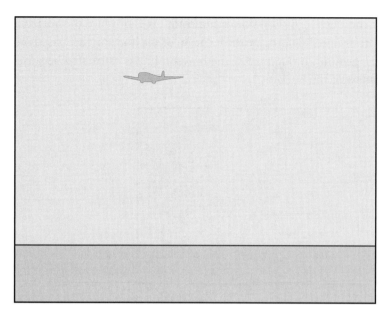

Figure 5.2
Looking up will lower the horizon line.

On the other hand, viewing a boat from a hillside will move the horizon line up, as shown in Figure 5.3.

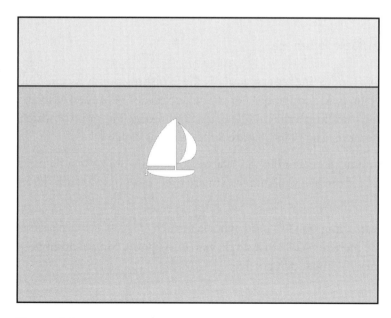

Figure 5.3
Looking down will raise the horizon line.

Sometimes objects in the scene, such as mountains or buildings, will obscure the horizon line. In these instances, the artist must determine the location of the horizon line based on the view and the slope of the ground. In Figure 5.4, the horizon line is estimated because the buildings block a clear view of the horizon.

Figure 5.4
The artist sometimes must estimate the horizon line.

Another concept that is important to linear perspective is the vanishing point. A *vanishing point* is the point on the horizon to which an object or character recedes. As a good example of a vanishing point, imagine standing in the middle of a straight road. The point at which the road meets the sky is the vanishing point. Figure 5.5 shows this concept.

You can use the vanishing point to determine the relative size of any object in a picture. In Figure 5.6, two lines drawn from the vanishing point are used as a guide for how large a character should be.

In this example, only one vanishing point is used. This is termed *single-point perspective* because all the objects in the picture recede to a single vanishing point. Single-point perspective is the most basic form of linear perspective.

Figure 5.5
The vanishing point is where the road meets the sky.

Figure 5.6
Lines from the vanishing point are used to determine the size of the character.

The most common type of linear perspective is two-point perspective. In *two-point perspective*, objects are defined by two separate vanishing points. Figure 5.7 shows an example of two-point perspective.

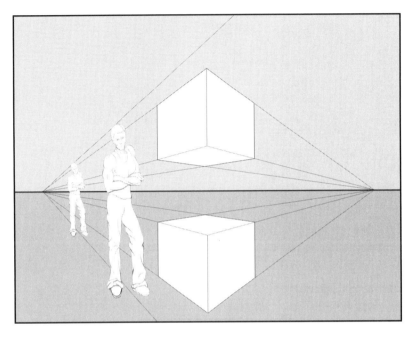

Figure 5.7
Two-point linear perspective uses two vanishing points to plot objects.

Two-point perspective adds to the realism of a picture because it allows more planes on the object to recede from view. Look at the difference between the cube in Figure 5.6 and the two cubes in Figure 5.7. In Figure 5.6, there is no way to plot the plane facing you with one vanishing point. This is okay if the plane facing the viewer is perpendicular to him or her, but it presents problems if there is even a slight rotation of view. With two-point perspective, the additional vanishing point makes it possible for an artist to draw an object from any angle.

Most objects in a picture are not always oriented to the same vanishing points. If the picture is of a city street, the building might line up with a similar or the same vanishing point, but other objects in the scene most likely will not. By changing the vanishing points for the objects in a scene, the artist is able to change their orientation to the viewer. Figure 5.8 shows several cubes with different vanishing points.

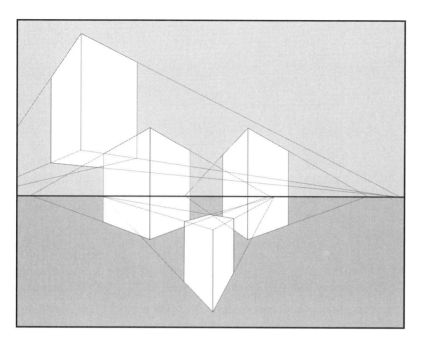

Figure 5.8
Most objects have their own vanishing points.

Two-point perspective will be adequate for an artist in most situations, but some situations will require even more accuracy. Notice that in two-point perspective, all of the vertical lines are parallel to each other. This isn't very obvious because often the convergences of these lines are so distant that you don't notice the difference.

Some objects are so massive that they look odd with only two-point perspective. In addition, extreme camera angles often call for more than a two-point approach. That is where three-point linear perspective comes into play. With the addition of a third point not connected to the horizon line, the artist is able to have the object recede from view correctly. Figure 5.9 shows how three-point perspective works. The cubes seem more massive with the addition of a third point.

Often the third point is some distance from the picture, as shown in Figure 5.9. To find the third point, the artist plots the angle of the center point of the object. Notice that in the case of Figure 5.9, the line goes directly up from the middle corner of the cube. The closer the third point is to the viewer, the more extreme the angle will appear. The other lines for the sides of the cube are then drawn down from the same point.

Linear perspective is a great tool, and I've only touched on it lightly in this book. You should take some time to study the subject in more detail.

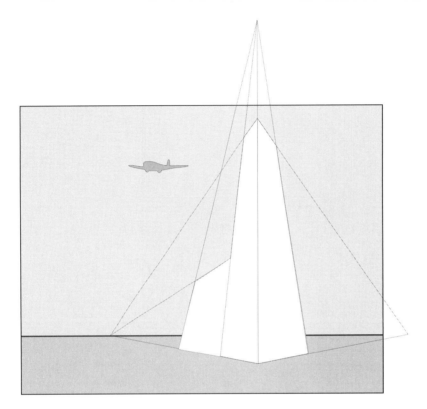

Figure 5.9
Three-point perspective helps to create extreme angles.

Composition

There are no hard rules in composition, only guidelines. For every rule, there is an example of an artist successfully breaking it. Rules in picture composition are a bit like spelling rules in the English language. They are guidelines you can use to help you create more pleasing pictures.

Unless the storyboard is for a cinematic, the design of the picture will be limited by the view of the game. Even with a cinematic sequence, there are some limitations on good camera movement, so all storyboards have limits on their design. Within those limits, however, the artist is free to use good design techniques in creating storyboards because those designs will carry through to the finished game.

Balance

Balance is basic to design. If a picture is out of balance, it will feel uncomfortable to the viewer. In Figure 5.10, the character is way off to the right and facing away from the center of the picture. This creates a large, uncomfortable, empty area in the middle and at the left side of the picture. In other words, the picture is off balance.

Figure 5.10
The picture is off balance.

A good way to think of picture balance is to imagine that the picture is perched on triangle. If the picture seems like it would be heavier on one side than on another, it will seem off balance (see Figure 5.11).

Figure 5.11
The picture is "heavier" on the right side, causing it to seem off balance.

One way to solve the balance problem is to use formal balance. *Formal balance* is a system of balancing a picture by subdividing it into equal portions so that one side mirrors the other. Formal balance feels comfortable to us because many things in life have symmetry. Most animals are symmetrical, as is the human body. For compositions in which the artist wishes to have a feeling of dignity or majesty, formal balance is a great approach. Figure 5.12 shows an example of how a picture can be subdivided to achieve a formal balance.

Figure 5.12
The lines show the formal balance of the composition.

Not everything needs to be mirrored from one side to the other, but there should be a sense of equality from one side to the other.

Formal balance is great for formal pictures, but because it is so balanced, the pictures can sometimes lack dynamics. Formal balance is not very good for creating pictures that give the feeling of motion or action, so the artist needs to have other ways to balance a picture.

Objects or characters in a composition don't have to be equal in size or mass to balance a picture. Artists can use the principle of the fulcrum lever in compositions. A *fulcrum lever* is like a seesaw. The center of the seesaw is the fulcrum. A heavier person can seesaw with a lighter person by moving closer to the fulcrum or having the lighter person move farther from the fulcrum. By placing a larger object or character near the center of the picture and placing the smaller object farther from the center, the picture will have a sense of balance. This approach to balance can add more drama to a picture. Figure 5.13 uses this method to balance the character in the foreground with the castle in the distance.

Figure 5.13
The fulcrum-lever approach can be used to balance a picture.

Focal Points

Every picture should have a focal point. A *focal point* is an area of a picture that attracts the primary interest of the viewer. Pictures with strong focal points are more pleasing to look at because they are not confusing to the viewer. Focal points can be achieved in several ways, including by using lines, values, detail, and color.

One of the most effective methods of creating a focal point is to use lines in the picture. Figure 5.14 shows how the lines of the picture converge on the castle, making it the focal point of the picture.

The lines in Figure 5.14 are not the straight lines overlaid; rather, they are part of the elements of the picture. The overlaid lines simply indicate the general direction of the elements. Organizing them to converge on a focal point is a design decision.

It is best not to place the focal point in the exact center of a picture because doing so can cause the picture to feel static. Shifting the focal point to one side or the other will help

Figure 5.14
The lines in the picture converge on the castle.

increase the dynamics of the arrangement. If the picture is a formal design, shifting the focal point to a position above center is usually the best choice.

Another excellent way to create a focal point is to use value. *Value* is the quality of light or dark in a picture. In Figure 5.15, the focal point is the silhouette of the knight on horseback.

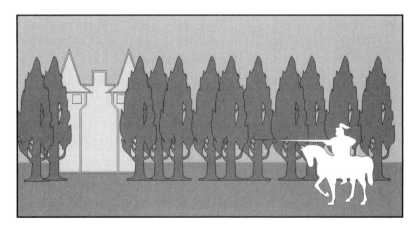

Figure 5.15
Value can be used to create a focal point.

To create a focal point using value, the artist places the highest contrast between light and dark at the focal point. All other images in the picture will have less contrast between light and dark.

Detail in a picture also will create a focal point. The eye is naturally drawn to areas of the picture that have greater detail. Figure 5.16 is a simple picture made up of mostly flat shapes. With the addition of a few lines of definition to the polo player, the eye is naturally drawn to the player, creating a focal point.

Figure 5.16
Detail can create a focal point.

Another very effective way to create a focal point is to use color. In Figure 5.17, the background is made of colors comprising variations from blue to red (although you can't see that in this book!). The trophy is a bright yellow, opposite the background colors on the color wheel. In this picture, it is the only color in the yellow family, which causes the viewer's eye to focus on it.

Most of the these examples are extreme to illustrate the different ways that lines, value, detail, and color can be used to focus the viewer's attention on a point on the picture. In practice, the artist should use judgment in the methods used to focus attention. The danger in being too heavy-handed with compositions is that when any technique or method of composition becomes too overbearing, the subject of the picture takes on less importance. Composition techniques should be used in such a way that they seem natural to the viewer, not contrived.

Figure 5.17
Color can be used to focus the viewer's attention.

Pathways

Artists can build pathways in a picture. When scanning a picture, the human eye moves about from one area of the picture to the next. If there are natural pathways in the picture, the viewer will be able to comfortably scan the picture. If the picture lacks natural pathways, it will feel uncomfortable to the viewer.

Figure 5.18 shows two pictures. The one on the top is the original storyboard sketch; the one on the bottom shows the paths of movement within the picture.

Shading

Shading is the process of adding value to a drawing. When you are drawing with a pencil on a white sheet of paper, shading is in only one direction. The white of the paper is the lightest area. Everything then becomes darker as more graphite is added to the drawing. The variation from light to dark in a drawing can be smooth or abrupt, depending on the subject and style of the artist.

Shading in a drawing is generally used to add volume and definition. In the case of a portrait like the one in Figure 5.19, the face is shaded using very gentle strokes to give it a smooth, subtle variation in value. The hair, on the other hand, received stronger, more direct strokes to help define the direction of the strands. The eyes have very abrupt changes in value.

Figure 5.18
Pictures should have natural paths of movement for the eye to follow.

Figure 5.19
Shading can be used to add volume and define detail in a picture.

Shading in a storyboard is usually one of the last steps an artist will take. When drawing a storyboard, the artist will generally rough in the idea using mostly lines with very little shading. Once a storyboard is roughed in and the artist is comfortable with the composition, it is a good idea to create a value sketch. A *value sketch* is a small thumbnail sketch that defines the light and dark areas of a picture without much detail. It is usually better to create a sketch small so the temptation to overwork the detail is minimized. Figure 5.20 shows the value sketch for the finished storyboard drawing shown in Figure 5.21. Notice how small it is compared to the finished drawing.

Figure 5.20
Make a value sketch before adding the shading to a picture.

Shading usually takes some time, so defining the areas in a small sketch helps to solve many of the design issues before the artist commits the time it will take to finish the drawing. Figure 5.21 shows the shaded storyboard.

Figure 5.21
Shading takes time, but sometimes it adds to the picture.

Creating the Storyboard

The first step in creating a storyboard panel is to draw some thumbnail pictures for each panel in the series. Because storyboards are used to describe an event, they usually will have two or more panels in a series. This series will have four panels to describe the hero-ine entering a room, discovering an enemy hidden in the room, defeating the enemy, and investigating the area where the enemy was hidden. Figure 5.22 shows the early thumbnail sketches for the series of panels.

Figure 5.22
The first step is to create thumbnails for each panel.

In the thumbnails, the artist works out the basic design of each panel. The game is a *third-person game*, meaning that the main character is viewed from behind and the player guides the character through the game. (A good example is Lara Croft in *Tomb Raider*.) This limits the design in many ways, but it is still possible to come up with some interesting compositions.

Once the artist is satisfied with the composition of each thumbnail sketch, work on the actual panel can commence. Figure 5.23 shows the storyboard panel roughed in very lightly.

It is important to not be too tight with the drawing in the initial stages. A looser, more fluid approach tends to help give the drawing a better feel. By not committing to any given line, the artist is able to feel the shapes as they are created. The loose initial drawing might change dramatically before the panel is finished, but drawing lightly helps get the artist past the blank sheet of paper that often stymies creativity.

Once the drawing is roughed in, the artist can then start refining the shapes. Figure 5.24 shows the drawing starting to take shape.

Notice that the lines are still relatively light. At this stage, the artist should still be searching for the right proportions of the figure and other objects in the environment. In this example, the perspective lines converge on the center of the heroine's back. This design element helps to center the viewer's attention on the main character in the panel.

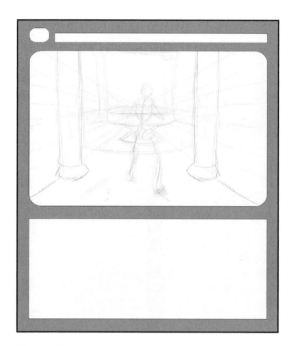

Figure 5.23
The initial panel is roughed in lightly.

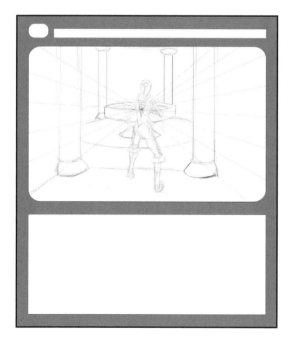

Figure 5.24
The shapes in the drawing are refined.

Once the major lines in the drawing are defined, the construction lines are then cleaned up as much as possible. Figure 5.25 shows the drawing in a more complete state, with most of the construction lines removed.

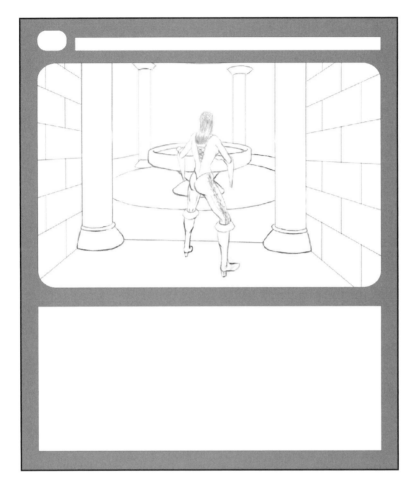

Figure 5.25
When the drawing is ready, the construction lines are removed.

hint

If you are using a digital drawing program, erasing and cleaning a drawing is not a problem. If you are using a pencil and paper, then you need to be very careful because erasing can cause damage to the surface of the paper, resulting in problems when you start shading.

After all the major lines of the drawing are in place, the artist can then start the shading process. At this point, it is usually a good idea to do a quick thumbnail sketch like the one in Figure 5.26 to define the values that will be used in the drawing.

Figure 5.26
Draw a quick thumbnail sketch to help define the values.

The final stage of the drawing is to add the shading. Shading a storyboard can be done with a pencil or with other media, such as markers, watercolor washes, or drawing pastels. The artist should experiment with different media to see what works best. Figure 5.27 shows the sketch with shading.

Figure 5.27
The last step is to add shading to the drawing.

The storyboard drawing is now complete, but the storyboard is not finished yet. The written information still needs to be added before the storyboard is finished. Figure 5.28 shows the completed storyboard with the written information.

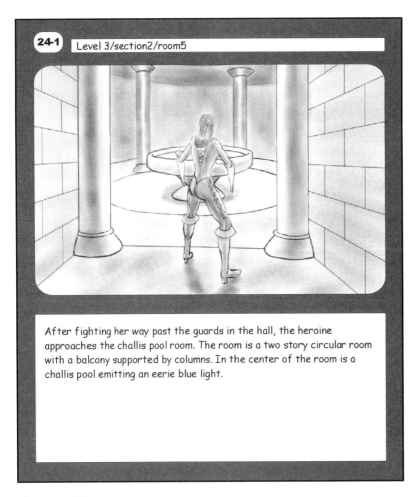

Figure 5.28
Finish the storyboard by adding the important written information.

Now that the first panel is finished, the artist can go on to the next panel in the series. Try drawing some of the remaining panels. You can use the thumbnails in Figure 5.22 as a starting point, or you can create your own.

Summary

This chapter covered many important topics related to storyboard drawing and drawing in general. Subsequent chapters will provide additional drawing instruction. Learning to draw well will greatly improve the concept artist's capability to make great storyboards. In this chapter, you should have learned the following concepts:

- Single-point linear perspective
- Two-point linear perspective
- Three-point linear perspective
- Composition balance
- Formal composition balance
- Fulcrum-lever balance
- Focal points
- Using lines to create focal points
- Using value to create focal points
- Using detail to create focal points
- Using color to create focal points
- Creating visual pathways in a composition
- The steps to creating a storyboard panel

Questions

1. What is a horizon line?
2. How do artists represent spatial relationships in pictures?
3. What is single-point perspective used for?
4. Which is more accurate, single-point or two-point perspective?
5. Are vanishing points always on the horizon line?
6. When should an artist use three-point perspective?
7. What is composition balance?
8. What composition technique creates a feeling of majesty?
9. Can a picture be balanced even if a larger object is placed off center?
10. What is the main focal point of a picture?
11. What four methods can an artist use to create a focal point?
12. How do lines in a picture create a focal point?
13. What is a pathway in a picture?
14. Why should the first lines of a storyboard be drawn lightly?
15. What should an artist do before shading a picture?

Answers

1. The line where the plane of the ground meets the sky.
2. By the using perspective.
3. Scenes in which all the lines recede to a single point on the horizon.
4. Two-point perspective.
5. No.
6. To show massive objects, such as tall buildings.
7. The feeling that a picture is not heavier on one side than the other.
8. Formal balance.
9. Yes, using the fulcrum-lever approach.
10. The natural center of interest.
11. Lines, value, detail, and color.
12. By converging on a single point in a picture.
13. Composition elements that guide the viewer's eye in a picture.
14. To give the artist greater freedom in creating the drawing.
15. Create a value sketch.

Discussion Questions

1. Why are good drawing skills important for creating good storyboards?
2. Why is perspective important in drawing storyboards?
3. Why should a picture be balanced?
4. How can an artist create focal points in a picture?
5. Why are pathways in art important?

Exercises

1. Create three pictures—one using single-point perspective, one using two-point perspective, and one using three-point perspective.
2. Find an example in which a great master artist created an off-balance picture. Explain why the picture was good even though it was off balance.
3. Create a set of storyboards with at least three panels to show how a character enters a room and reacts to the characters inside.

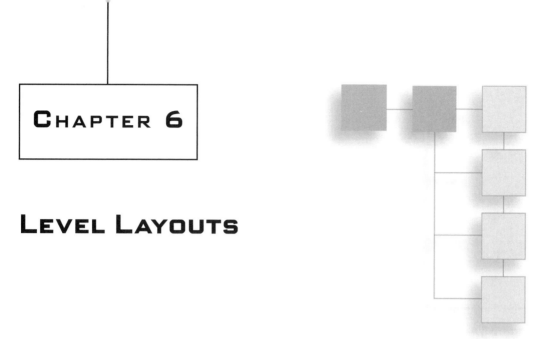

CHAPTER 6

LEVEL LAYOUTS

L evel layouts are the road maps to the levels in a game. They are used to define and organize the elements in levels. This chapter will explore level design and show you how level layouts are used in the creation of a game. It will include a discussion of what level layouts are and how they are used in game development. It will also cover the information that should be in a level layout, as well as how to create a level layout.

What Are Level Layouts?

A *level layout* is a scale drawing of a level used as a guide by the development team to create a level in a game. Level layouts are drawn to scale because they need to be accurate. The development team will be using them as guides, so the more accurate the drawings are, the better the development team will be able to create the vision of the game design.

Unlike other concept art, level layouts are not concerned with artistic composition. They are working drawings, so the main focus is on clarity and communication. The actual items in the level will determine the composition, not any particular artistic design. This isn't to say that the drawing doesn't have to look good; it just means that the artist needs to focus on the needs of the game, not on the composition of the picture.

When creating a level layout, the paramount consideration is developing a fun game. All elements in the layout should be placed to create a fun experience for the player. For example, if a game is a side-view platform game, the distance a character can jump is important. Figure 6.1 shows a section of a level layout for a platform game.

The character's jumping distances are shown with dotted lines. The large vertical shaft in the center of the drawing is too wide for the character to jump unaided. A springboard placed at the edge of the shaft can propel the character over the shaft if he makes a running

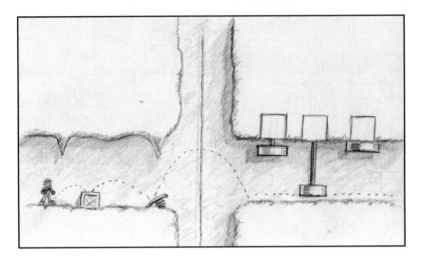

Figure 6.1
Jumping distances are shown with dotted lines.

jump from the crate. Notice the stalactites along the roof of the cave. If the player times the jumps incorrectly, the character is likely to hit one of those. Once he is over the shaft, the player will need to stop the character's forward momentum or risk being smashed by the pistons. In this section, the character has to time his movement to avoid being crushed.

From this example, it should be evident that the level layout defines the level in great detail. Level layouts are usually collaborations between the game designer and the concept artist. The designer will sometimes create rough sketches on graph paper, which the artist must interpret into the layouts.

How Level Layouts Are Used in Game Creation

Because level layouts contain extensive detail, they are used for many purposes in the course of game creation. The most common, of course, is to convey the level designs to the development team. Another equally important use of level layouts is to determine the assets for the game. In addition, layouts are used to define story elements, place characters and objects, locate events, and define paths.

Creating Level Designs

When creating a level, the development team builds all the elements that go into it. The development team will use the level layouts as templates to create the levels. Figure 6.2 shows a level layout for a racing game.

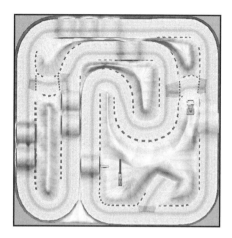

Figure 6.2
Layouts for levels need to be accurate.

The layout is rendered to show the hills and jumps on the track. In Figure 6.3, the layout is used as a template to guide the development artist in creating the track. Notice the wire-frame model above the track. It shows how the model was created from the original layout.

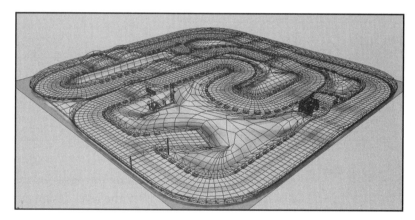

Figure 6.3
The layout is used as a template.

The model will not always follow the layout exactly because there will always need to be game adjustments. However, the layout is the base for the model, and without it the development team would have no concrete guidelines for developing the game worlds.

Determining Asset Count

Building games is expensive. One of the major costs is the creation of all the game assets. *Game assets* are the graphics and audio work used in creating the game. This includes the game worlds, characters, objects, vehicles, creatures, weapons, effects, and all audio files. Basically, any art or audio files used in the creation of the game are considered game assets, even if they are not actually used in the final version of the game. Costs for creating game assets can run in the millions. Therefore, it is important to be able to predict the amount of assets a game will require before you begin development.

The level layout is a tool to help the game designer come up with an asset list to include in the final design. The painstaking detail of a level layout is ideal for determining the number and complexity of graphics and audio files necessary for each level. All the designer needs to do is go over the layout and write down all the game elements. For this reason, a level layout needs to include everything in a level.

Level layouts will generally contain a legend that describes elements in the layout. Figure 6.4 shows a safari game. A legend on the side of the layout gives more specific information about the symbols used in the layout. A *legend* is a written list that corresponds to symbols or other art used in a layout.

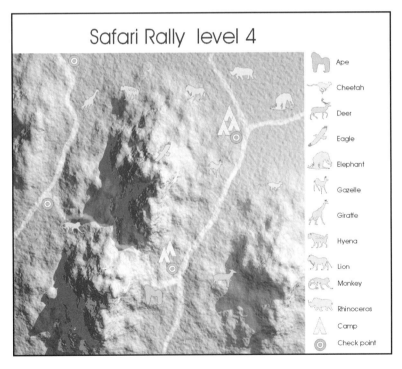

Figure 6.4
The legend gives more specific information about layout elements.

Defining the Story

Many games have story elements. The level layout is where the designer orchestrates the progression of the story. In a level layout, the designer can plan for the regulation of the game, plan story elements, and create a series of events that will propel the story forward in the game. For instance, if the game is about finding a buried treasure, the designer can give the player clues throughout the game. The clues are placed in the level layout in such a way that the player has to discover each one in order to solve the mystery of the treasure's location.

The designer can limit access to some areas of the game based on the completion of a specific event. In the game layout, the designer can place an event that will trigger another event, and then refer to both in the legend to show that one thing has to happen before another.

Placing Characters and Objects

The game layout will indicate locations of characters and objects. As part of the game layout, the designer will indicate where a character or object will be located. It is important to place the characters and objects in the level layout because they are the interactive features of the game. If the game is a military game, for example, the placement of enemy forces is critical to the game play. If there are too many enemy soldiers in a location, the player will not be able to defeat them. If there are too few soldiers, the player will not have any challenge. With a level layout, the designer has a visual way to determine whether the characters are placed too close together.

Placing Events

Events are also placed in a game layout. An *event* is something that will happen that affects the game. For example, a mystery game might have a clue to a murder that is only available after the player talks to a specific character and asks a specific question. The asking of the question is a game event that triggers another game event. These events can be added as symbols in the layout, and then described in the layout legend.

Other events might be environmental changes. A golf game might have a random occurrence of rain on any given hole. The event is a random rain trigger, and it should be included in the level with information on how it works.

There are any number of events that happen in a game. Defining them in the level layout is the best way to keep track of them. In the layout, the designer is able to see to it that no one area is too overcrowded with events, while other areas have none.

Defining Paths

The designer can use level layouts to define the path of a player through the game. *Game paths* are the possible ways a player can move through a game. Some games are very open and allow the player to wander about with no real path of progression. These games are called *open path games*. Other games are very tightly controlled and give the player few choices in game progression. These games are referred to as *linear games*.

Game paths are often defined in the level layout. For example, in a fantasy game the player might need to have a certain level of armor to protect him from the dragon's attack. The designer can set up the game so that the player has to go through a canyon to reach the dragon's cave. Along the way to the cave, the player might discover the bones of an ancient warrior. The needed armor is there for the taking. Thus, the designer has created a path to the dragon that crosses a necessary event. The canyon is the path.

There are many ways to create paths in a game. Paths can be set in stone so the player has very little choice, or they can be very open and flexible, with the guidance as suggestions rather than commands. In the case of the dragon and the canyon, the player has no choice for killing the dragon except going through the canyon. In another game, the dragon's cave might be approachable from any number of directions, leaving it up the player how he will approach it.

Information in Level Layouts

Level layouts contain extensive information about the specifics of a given level. To create a good level, the designer must visualize the game and play it in his mind. Each important facet of the game needs to be recorded. The level layout is where the designer records the information.

Level layouts are ideal for storing information because they are both a visual and a written document. The visual aspects of the document allow the designer to place things in a game by location. The items placed can be actual objects or characters seen in the game, or they can be elements that are not seen in the game but that still have an effect on it, such as events. The written portion of the document describes the items placed in the layout and allows the designer to add the element of time.

A level layout is a detailed document. The more information it contains, the better the development process will be because less will be left to chance. In the layout, the designer creates a paper version of the game and works out many of the problems. The layout gives the designer a chance to see the game in a special format so the game play can be balanced.

The previous chapter introduced the concept of compositional balance. Like composition, games need to be balanced as well. A balanced game is more fun to play because the game elements are not crowded in one area while another area is vacant. The game progresses in a natural way. The challenges in the game are within the scope of the player's skill, and the game does not have glaring flaws that allow the player to circumvent important game aspects. In the level layout, the designer can work on balancing the game on paper before it is put into production.

Creating a Level Layout

The first step in creating a level layout is defining the area that the level will include. For this example, assume the game level will be the top floor of a hunting lodge. The lodge will have many guests that the player will need to meet and talk to during the course of the game. The top floor of the lodge needs to contain a secret room, a library, a lounge, a piano room, a bathroom, a kitchen, and some guest rooms.

Start by drawing a rectangle that will define the outer dimensions of the level, as shown in Figure 6.5.

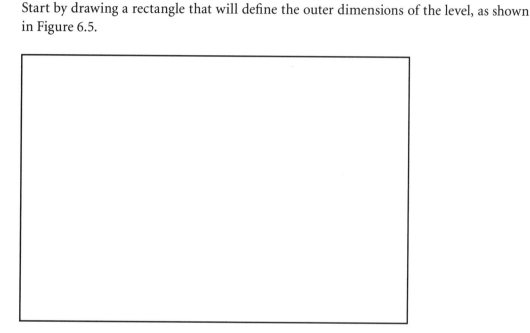

Figure 6.5
Define the size of the level by drawing a rectangle.

This level layout will look very similar to a simple floor plan. Not all level layouts will look like floor plans, but thinking of them as such can be very useful because the game developers will use these layouts to construct the level, much like a construction team would use a floor plan to construct a house.

Next, draw in the rooms, as shown in Figure 6.6. You can draw smaller guest rooms at the top of the drawing and larger common rooms in the lower part of the drawing. You should also include openings for doors.

This is the upper floor of the hunting lodge. The players need a way to get their characters from the bottom floor to the top floor. You can add a staircase to the right side of the drawing, as shown in Figure 6.7.

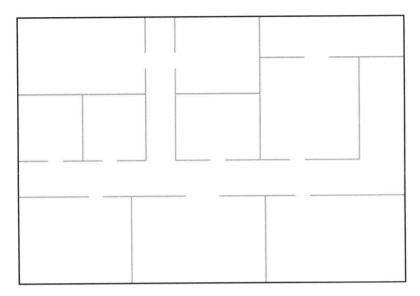

Figure 6.6
Draw in the walls of the upper floor.

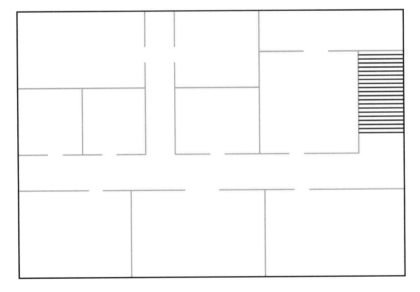

Figure 6.7
Add a staircase to the right side of the layout.

All good hunting lodges need doors, so you should add doors to each room. When you are creating objects that are duplicates of each other, such as doors, you don't have to create each one individually. Drawing programs, such as Adobe Illustrator and CorelDRAW, allow you to create an object and replicate it as many times as needed. If you create the drawing by hand, you can build an object and then use a copy machine to create several identical copies that can be pasted onto the drawing. Another option is to cut a template from a heavy piece of cardstock and use it as a drawing guide. Figure 6.8 shows the door object. It is created with two heavy lines to show its open and closed positions. A lighter line arches from the heavier lines to show the door's swing.

Figure 6.8
The door symbol is made up of three lines.

Figure 6.9 shows the doors for all the rooms, including the secret door to the secret room. Notice that all the doors are symbols, but they are still drawn to scale.

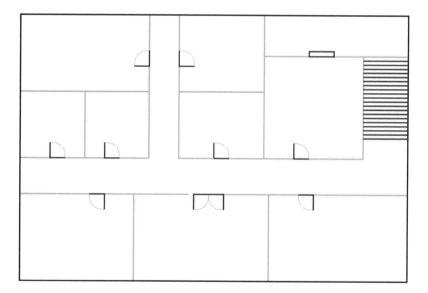

Figure 6.9
Add the doors to the drawing.

The next step is to put furniture in the room. Many drawing programs have symbols in their font libraries for floor plans. In addition, you can purchase symbols from your local architectural supply store. Figure 6.10 shows the piano room with some couches, a chair, and a few other furnishings. The symbols are all part of the symbol library in a drawing program. If you want to create your own furniture items, you can do so in the same way as you created the door. Even when you are using symbols, the items need to be scaled to accurately fit the layout.

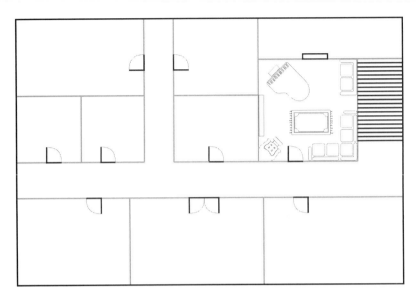

Figure 6.10
Add furniture to one of the rooms.

The rooms in the upper portion of the drawing are mostly guest rooms, and several have beds. The secret room is located just above the piano room, where it will be difficult for the player to detect in relation to the other rooms. Figure 6.11 shows these rooms added to the layout.

Continue to add furniture to the rest of the lodge, as shown in Figure 6.12.

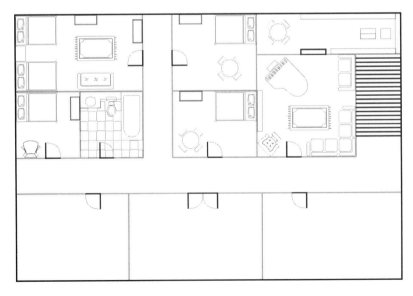

Figure 6.11
Add furniture to the rooms in the upper portion of the layout.

Figure 6.12
Furnish each room in the level.

The lodge needs a floor to keep the characters from falling to the level below. Add a floor under the furniture by lightly drawing lines to indicate hardwood flooring. With a floor in place, you also can add some shadows to give the layout more depth, as shown in Figure 6.13.

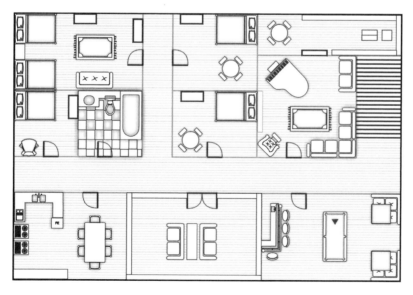

Figure 6.13
Add a floor and some shading.

This game is an adventure game. The player must interview other people in the level to get information. The next step in the level layout is to add the characters. Again, you can create a symbol to represent each character. Figure 6.14 shows the characters added to the layout.

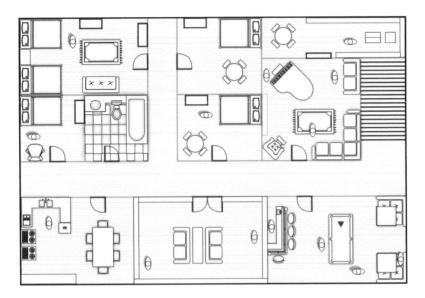

Figure 6.14
The characters are added to the layout.

You should number the characters and add a list of the characters to the layout (see Figure 6.15). The list is the layout legend.

Some games will have characters and objects that need to be listed in the layout legend. The legend is the numbered list next to the picture. It can contain any important game information. Figure 6.16 shows the addition of the objects.

Notice that only numbers are added to the layout for the objects. Drawing an object that is too small to be seen in a scale drawing is a wasted effort. Usually a number and description in the legend are sufficient.

The level layout is now finished and ready to add to the design document. The only things not included in the layout at this stage are events. If necessary, these can be added the same way the objects were.

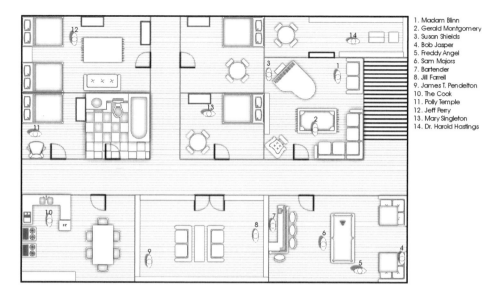

Figure 6.15
Numbers are added to identify the characters.

Figure 6.16
The objects are added to the layout and the legend.

Summary

This chapter contained many important issues about the creation of level layouts. In this chapter, you should have learned the following concepts:

- What level layouts are
- How level layouts are used
- Using layouts as templates
- Using layouts to create asset lists
- Using layouts to direct the game story
- Using layouts to place characters and objects
- Using layouts to place events
- Using layouts to define paths
- The information that should be included in a level layout
- How to create a level layout

You should now be familiar with the basic structure of a level layout, including how one is created and used in game designs.

Questions

1. What is a level layout?
2. Is artistic composition important in level layouts?
3. Are clarity and accuracy important in level layouts?
4. How should elements in a level layout be placed?
5. True or false: Level layouts need not be detailed drawings.
6. What is the most common use for a level layout?
7. Should the level layout be accurate enough that the development team can use it for a template when creating the game world?
8. True or false: Creating game assets is not a major cost factor in game development.
9. What makes a great tool for coming up with an asset list?
10. What is the numbered list called in a level layout?
11. What can a game designer do to keep a player out of an area until a certain event occurs?
12. True or false: Character placement is an important part of level layouts.
13. True or false: Because events are not seen, they are not usually part of a level layout.

14. What is it called when a designer defines the movement through a level?

15. What does the designer need to do to make sure the game does not have too many events in one area and not enough in another?

Answers

1. A scale drawing of a level used as a guide by the development team to create a level in a game.

2. No.

3. Yes.

4. To create a fun experience for the player.

5. False.

6. To convey the level design to the development team.

7. Yes.

8. False.

9. Level layouts.

10. The legend.

11. Limit access to the area.

12. True.

13. False.

14. Defining the game path.

15. Balance the game.

Discussion Questions

1. Why are level layouts important?

2. Why is it important to understand how many assets are needed in a game?

3. How can a designer use a level layout to set up a story?

4. Why is a balanced game better than an unbalanced game?

5. Why is it important to define the overall size of a level as the first step in creating a level layout?

Exercises

1. Create a level layout for a side-view platform game. Make the level fun by adding several unique game elements for the player to navigate.

2. Create a level layout for a racing game. Make the course interesting by adding several jumps and other terrain features.

3. Map out a level from a favorite game and create a level layout from your map.

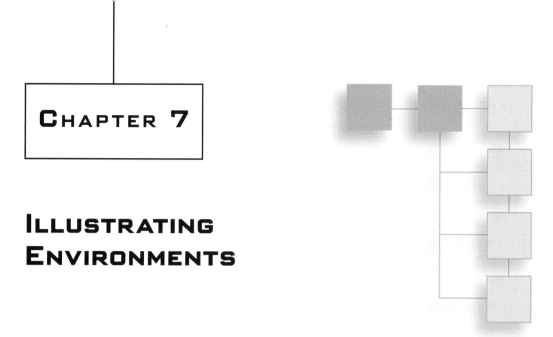

CHAPTER 7

ILLUSTRATING ENVIRONMENTS

The environment illustration is one of the most creative areas of concept art creation. Unlike level layouts or storyboards, the environment illustration is not constrained by the need for painstaking accuracy. It is an illustration of the game world designed to give the development team a feeling for the mood and nature of a particular area. This is not to say that there is no need for accuracy in an environment sketch or illustration; it is simply to say the need for accuracy is not as high because its purpose is different.

This chapter will explore the uses and purposes of environment sketches and illustrations in game development. It will also give step-by-step examples for creating an environment sketch (a black-and-white drawing of an environment) and an environment illustration (a full-color rendering of an environment).

What Is an Environment Illustration?

An *environment illustration* is a detailed picture of an area of the game world. It is usually taken from the same view that the player will see the game, but it can also be an overview of the world. In reality, an environment illustration is a painting of the game world, as if the concept artist set up an easel and painted the scene.

The size and detail of environment illustrations vary. Some are large and expansive, showing a large area of a game level, similar to a panorama. Others are intimate, showing a small view or a single item in the level. Some have extensive detail, while others have little specific detail and instead show more of the mood of the area.

Uses and Purposes of Environment Illustrations

Environment sketches and illustrations are used to inspire and give direction to the development team. The concept artist will not be able to illustrate every area in a level; it would take hundreds of illustrations to define every area in a game. Rather, the artist's job is to capture the mood and feeling of an area, and then let the development team artists expand it to cover the entire level.

Inspiration

The environment illustration is best when it is an inspirational work of art. The more the concept artist can capture the feel of an area in the illustration, the better the development team will be able to interpret that feeling throughout the level. This is one of the main reasons why environment illustration is more creative than other concept art. Art for inspiration is very different than art for information.

When creating an inspirational piece, the artist must first determine the mood and character of the area he needs to depict. For example, if the game is a cartoon-style platform game, the artist shouldn't try to create a realistic, highly detailed illustration. Rather, the illustration should convey the feeling of the finished game. On the other hand, if the game is a horror survival game, the artist should not create the concept art in a cartoon style.

When creating inspirational work, it is helpful if the artist is inspired first. A good way to gain inspiration is to become immersed in the best examples of art available for the type of game being designed. Look at other games in the same genre to see what has been done in the past. If there are any good movies in the genre of the game, view them to see what the Hollywood artists are doing.

Perhaps the best inspiration of all is to look at great art. Look at the masterpieces of the great artists of the past. Nothing inspires quite like great art. A little study of art history will pay big dividends to any concept artist. A quick trip to a museum is a great way to help an artist begin to put together some ideas for game levels. If there are no museums in the area, spend some time on the Internet or looking at art history books.

Direction

Although inspiration is a major part of an environment illustration, it is not the only purpose. In many areas of a level, specific items or scenery will be needed in the game. Environment illustrations can show the development team a specific area or item. For example, if the game is a futuristic adventure game and the design calls for a special kind of force field around a quest item, it would be much easier to show the field in an illustration than to describe it. With the illustration, the chance of error in creating the force field is also greatly reduced.

The concept artist works with the designer to come up with a vision for each area in the game. Using the level layout, the designer and concept artist identify the areas that need to be illustrated. Each level will need at least one illustration to set its mood. The other illustrations are based on the need to give specific information to the development team, as in the aforementioned example.

Some levels might have more than one type of area. A level might have a large, seemingly abandoned warehouse, but inside one area of the warehouse there might be a lush living area for a drug dealer. In situations like this, the concept artist must create an environment illustration for each unique area in the level.

Some levels may change. There might be weather effects in a racing game, for example, or the level's appearance might change depending on the time of day. The concept artist should create an illustration for how the level might change so the development team can implement the changes.

Creating an Environment Sketch

Environment sketches are black-and-white drawings of an area in a level. They are used primarily where specific information is needed but color is not. An environment sketch takes much less time to create than a color illustration.

The following example is a sketch of an area in a tropical rainforest. The main character is in a jungle. The location is near a vine-covered statue from an ancient building. The statue is a clue to the player. To get the statue to look right, the concept artist must create a sketch to show the development team.

The first step in creating the sketch is to rough in the drawing lightly to define the major elements. Draw a few thumbnail sketches, and then take the best design and start drawing. Figure 7.1 shows the roughed-in drawing. The drawing at this stage is still very loose and

Figure 7.1
Lightly rough in the composition of the drawing.

free. All that is needed is definition of the composition and content of the picture. Notice the composition lines that converge on the character. Unlike in other types of concept art, in environment sketches and illustrations the artist is freer to use composition techniques.

Once the framework for the drawing is laid, the rendering can begin. Figure 7.2 shows the beginning of the rendering. In this example, the statue is detailed using a directional stroke to give it the feeling of old, weathered stone covered by vines.

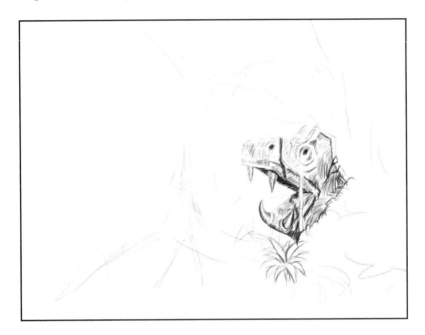

Figure 7.2
Start to render the elements in the drawing.

The two major points of interest in the drawing are the main character and the ancient statue. Define these two elements, and then add the other parts of the drawing (see Figure 7.3).

Continue to move from section to section of the picture, defining the vegetation and other jungle elements, as shown in Figure 7.4. The lower-right quadrant of the picture is beginning to take shape. Some artists prefer to work on the entire picture at once, developing all the areas together. In this example, the drawing is developed section by section. Either way is fine as long as the initial construction lines are in and the artist has done a value sketch, as discussed in Chapter 5.

Figure 7.3
Define the main character and the statue.

Figure 7.4
Continue to work on different sections of the picture.

The picture is of a path through the jungle. The jungle is a lush rainforest area, so the picture needs to define that in the viewer's mind. Add detail to the sides of the path so the development team can see the types of plants that are needed in the game (see Figure 7.5).

Figure 7.5
Add detail to the path.

The drawing is starting to take shape. Much of the foliage is now in the picture, and it is starting to feel like an enclosed, thickly wooded area. Figure 7.6 shows the picture as it nears completion.

Figure 7.7 shows the nearly completed picture. The development team should be able to get a good idea of how the game will look in this area from the drawing.

Figure 7.6
Continue to add detail to the picture's background.

Figure 7.7
The nearly finished drawing

The last few things to add to the drawing are the distant tree line, some more definition to the mid-ground foliage, and some shading around the character to bring her out more. Figure 7.8 shows the finished sketch.

Figure 7.8
Add the final touches to finish the sketch.

Environment sketches are great for most tasks, but they don't give the design team any color information. Full-color illustrations are best for that.

Using Color

Before I go into an example of creating a full-color illustration of an environment, I want to explain a bit about color. One of the most noticeable characteristics of any surface is its color. People often refer to an object by its color. They might refer to the red car or the blue sweater. Some colors have emotional ties. A person who is on a lucky streak might be called "red-hot," while a person who is depressed is often called "blue." We even assign temperatures to colors. Red, yellow, and orange are considered warm colors, while purple, blue, and green are thought of as cool colors.

How Light Affects Colors

To better understand color, it is important to first look at light. When pure light strikes an object, some of the light energy is absorbed and some is reflected. The light that is seen is what is reflected. For example, when light strikes a red object, the object absorbs the other bands of light and reflects to us only the red light.

The human eye can only discern a narrow band of the full spectrum of light. That light is called the *visible band* of light, and it is made up of a spectrum of colors. A rainbow is an example of the spectrum of visible light. Rainbows are made from light bouncing off water particles in the air. Because each color has its own unique characteristics, some colors are bounced in one direction and some are bounced in another, forming bands of pure color. These bands of color are always in the same order, with red at one end and violet or purple at the other end. All the rest of the colors are between those two colors.

Pure light is often called *white light*. White light contains the full spectrum of colors, so white objects reflect all of the colors of the spectrum. Black, on the other hand, absorbs all of the colors of the spectrum. A black object absorbs the full spectrum of light, while a white object reflects the full spectrum of light. That is why black objects tend to heat more when placed in the light, while white objects tend to heat less.

Understanding light is very important to understanding how color works. Unless you are in a completely dark room, every object sends light to your eyes. This light not only affects the object itself, but also other objects around it. Try an experiment: Place a white card next to a bright-red object. You can see the red light from the object bouncing off the white of the card. The effect is similar to shining a red light on the card, but it is not as pronounced. Figure 7.9 illustrates how light bounces off a red object.

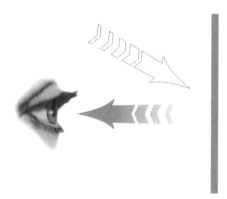

Figure 7.9
When white light strikes a red object, only red light is reflected.

Any light you see that is not pure is missing part of the full spectrum of color. In some ways, you can call colored light *deficient light*. Because colored light is deficient in one or more bands of color, it affects the objects it lights. Because red light does not contain blue light, objects that are blue in normal light will look very different in red light. This principle holds true for all colored light.

Using the Color Wheel

A common tool for artists is a *color wheel*—an ordered placement of colors in a circle based on their relative position in the full spectrum of light. Remember that one end of the bands of color on a rainbow is red, and the other is purple or violet. On a color wheel, these two colors are next to each other, and the other colors are arranged around the circle in order. Figure 7.10 shows a simple color wheel.

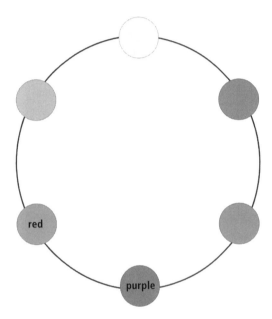

Figure 7.10
Red and purple are next to each other on the color wheel.

The color wheel has many purposes beyond just organizing the colors of the spectrum. Red, blue, and yellow on a color wheel represent *primary colors*. They are considered primary because they are pure bands of colors, not mixtures of other colors (see Figure 7.11).

Orange is a mixture of yellow and red; therefore, it is not a primary color. Colors that are even mixtures of primary colors are called *secondary colors*. These colors are orange, green, and purple (see Figure 7.12).

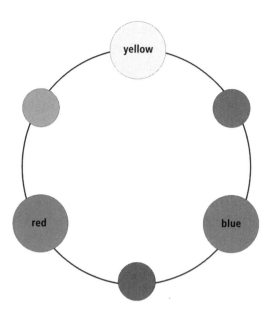

Figure 7.11
Red, blue, and yellow are primary colors.

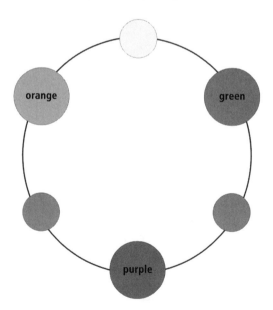

Figure 7.12
Orange, green, and purple are secondary colors.

Opposite colors on the color wheel are called *complimentary colors* because if they are placed next to each other, each color will tend to look bolder. Complimentary colors generally do not work well placed next to each other in a picture. They tend to amplify each other, giving the picture a feeling of clashing colors. Unless you are trying to make the picture uncomfortable, you should avoid placing complimentary colors next to each other. Figure 7.13 shows two complimentary colors—red and green.

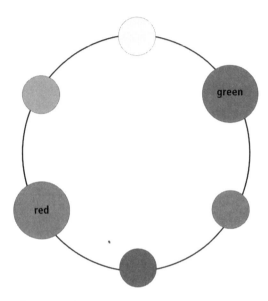

Figure 7.13
Red and green are opposite each other in the color wheel.

Colors that are next to each other on the color wheel are called *analogous colors* (see Figure 7.14). These colors tend to fit nicely next to each other in pictures, perhaps because they are next to each other in the natural spectrum.

hint

Most people like the way the colors of the rainbow blend into each other. When placing colors in a picture, it is often more pleasing to go around the color wheel from one color to the next. For example, if there is something in the picture that is red and something next to it that is blue, placing a little purple between the two colors gives the picture a more pleasant feeling.

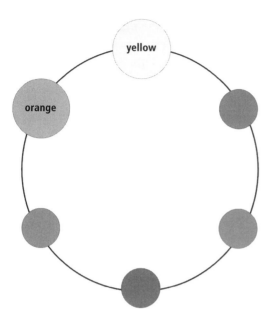

Figure 7.14
Analogous colors, such as orange and yellow, are next to each other on the color wheel.

Creating an Environment Illustration

The first step for creating an environment illustration is the same as the first step for creating any drawing or painting. The artist needs to rough in the basic composition of the picture. Figure 7.15 shows the beginnings of the drawing that will lay the foundation for the painting.

Figure 7.15
Block in the basic areas of the drawing.

Because this will be a painting rather than a drawing, most of the detail is reserved for later. The drawing acts as a guide for the artist to help with the major shapes. Some areas will require a higher degree of detail than others. The main character, for example, is defined more than the background (see Figure 7.16).

Figure 7.16
Define the main character.

The next step is to add color to the painting. The colors are laid down loosely with an airbrush to define each major part of the painting. Notice the sky goes from yellow on the right side of the screen to blue on the left. Rather than going through green (around the color wheel) the sky transitions around the color wheel the other direction, through red. Figure 7.17 shows the basic colors of the picture. Although you can't see the actual colors in the book, you can get an idea of what has been airbrushed. (You can see the illustration in color on the CD-ROM that comes with this book.)

When painting, there are a lot of methods you can use to work on a picture. In this example, the background elements are painted in first, moving toward the foreground. Figure 7.18 shows the clouds added to the picture. Notice how the cloud on the right acts as a design element, pointing toward the main character.

Figure 7.17
Block in the general shapes in color.

Figure 7.18
Add clouds to the picture.

One of the best reasons to move from the back to the front is because you can maintain better edges. The background elements can go over the area of the foreground. Later, when the foreground elements are painted in, the artist can establish the edge between the foreground and background. This only works with opaque media. If the artist is working in a transparent medium, such as watercolors, the edges have to be painted exactly.

Figure 7.19 shows the progress of the painting, with the distant mountains and some of the mid-ground elements.

Figure 7.19
Paint from the back to the front.

When working on a specific object in the picture, the first things an artist should consider are the basic values that will be used in the object. In Figure 7.20, the arch is first defined with the light side and the shadow side.

Once the basic values are applied, it is much easier to add the detail. In Figure 7.21, the detail of the cracked stone is added. Notice that the light side of the arch picks up the yellow from the sun, and the shadow side picks up some of the cooler colors from the left side of the picture.

Figure 7.20
Paint the basic values first.

Figure 7.21
Add detail to the arch.

This painting uses a technique called aerial perspective to achieve depth. *Aerial perspective* is a technique in which objects tend to be less defined and have less contrast the farther they are from the viewer. In nature, when an object gets farther away, there is more atmosphere between the object and the viewer. The atmosphere might contain dust or water particles that can obscure a clear view of the object. The more particles there are in the air, the more pronounced the effect becomes. A good example of aerial perspective is how things look on a foggy day. If the fog is very thick, very little is seen. As the fog clears, you can see farther away.

Now that the background is finished, it is time to move on to the foreground elements. As the objects get closer to the viewer, each element is given more contrast. The darks become darker, and the highlights become lighter. This enhances the feeling of aerial perspective. Figure 7.22 shows some of the foreground elements painted in.

Figure 7.22
The foreground elements have greater contrast than the background elements.

Completing the detail in the foreground finishes the painting. The greatest detail and contrast are in the main character in the lower-center portion of the picture. He becomes the focal point of the painting, as shown in Figure 7.23.

Figure 7.23
The figure becomes the focal point of the picture.

The finished picture can now be added to the game design. The painting establishes the colors in the level and a mood of ancient, decaying grandeur with the arch. It also gives the development team a sense of scale by comparing the arch with the character in the foreground.

Summary

This chapter was primarily about creating environment illustrations; however, it also introduced some basic concepts of color. In this chapter, you should have learned the following concepts:

- What environment sketches are
- What environment illustrations are
- How environment illustrations are used in game development
- Why environment illustrations offer more design freedom than other concept art
- How you see color
- What the color wheel is
- What colors go well together
- What aerial perspective is

- How to create an environment sketch
- How to create an environment illustration

Questions

1. Why are environment illustrations more creative than other concept art?
2. Does mood play a role in an environment sketch?
3. What are some good sources of inspiration for creating environment illustrations?
4. Besides inspiration, what else are environment illustrations used for?
5. Should every level of a game have an environment illustration?
6. Why might an artist create more than one environment illustration of the same area?
7. Who generally determines the areas of a level that need environment illustrations?
8. Do environment sketches generally have color?
9. What are environment sketches used for?
10. What colors are absorbed by red objects?
11. What are the secondary colors?
12. Is it usually a good idea to place complimentary colors next to each other?
13. Is it usually a good idea to place analogous colors next to each other?
14. Why is it a good idea to paint from the background forward in a painting when you are using opaque media?
15. What kind of perspective is created by more contrast and detail in foreground objects?

Answers

1. There is not as much need for accuracy.
2. Yes.
3. Other games, movies, and great works of art.
4. To show details of objects or areas that the design team wants to communicate to the development team.
5. Yes.
6. The level might change during the game.
7. The designer and the concept artist.
8. No.
9. Mostly to show detail in an area of a level.
10. All of them except red.

11. Green, purple, and orange.

12. No.

13. Yes.

14. It helps you create better edges.

15. Aerial perspective.

Discussion Questions

1. What are environment illustrations?

2. How are environment illustrations used in game development?

3. What are some good ways for artists to get inspiration?

4. Why is understanding the color wheel useful in painting?

5. How can an artist use aerial perspective to create interesting pictures?

Exercises

1. Create an environment illustration of an interior of a throne room. Give enough detail to the throne that the development team will be able to create it in the game.

2. Using colors from your own palette, create a color wheel and place each color where it belongs on the wheel. Explain why you may or may not have a good palette of colors.

3. Create an environment illustration of a racing game that shows the finish line. Try to give the illustration a dramatic feeling.

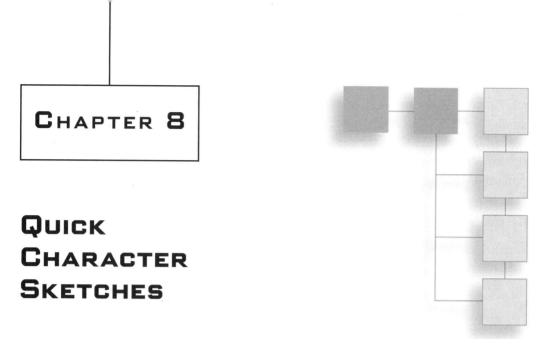

CHAPTER 8

QUICK CHARACTER SKETCHES

C reating good game characters is one of the most important aspects of concept art. Like the actors and actresses in a motion picture, characters are the focus of attention in a game. It is the job of the concept artist to create great characters.

The next two chapters deal with creating characters for games. This chapter deals with characters sketches and character development and covers basic drawing skills as they relate to character creation. Chapter 9, "Creating Character Illustrations," focuses more on creating character designs for the design document.

This chapter will cover what game characters are and the types of characters found in games. It will also give you some helpful suggestions for getting inspiration for characters, and it will explain how to draw characters.

Game Characters

With the possible exception of some puzzle games, almost every game has characters. In fact, many puzzle games even have characters. Often games have the player control a character in the game. Some games even allow the player to create a character to play in the game.

Game characters include all intelligent people or creatures in a game. *Intelligent* means that the character is controlled by either the player or the game software. The specific software that controls characters in games is called *artificial intelligence*, or *AI* for short. AI in games is becoming increasingly complex, to the point that the player can interact with AI-controlled characters as if the characters were real.

When game characters first started appearing in games, they were only vague representations of people or creatures. There isn't a lot that an artist can do when the game character is only 16 pixels high. Advances in technology have led to an increase in character size and complexity.

Characters in games are also becoming more and more lifelike, to the point that they don't only run around and shoot things—they can also have emotion. An angry character will not simply attack with sword drawn; he will also use facial expressions and body language to emphasize the attack. Characters in games can display a full range of emotions. This greater sophistication has increased the demands on designers and concept artists to develop interesting and engaging characters.

Types of Game Characters

Some games have many different types of characters, while others are simpler in their approach to characters. The following is a list of categories into which game characters can be broken:

- Player characters
- Non-player characters
- Enemies

Each of the items on the list has one or more subcategories. Player characters can be broken down into the characters controlled by one player and characters controlled by other players. Non-player characters (or NPCs, for short) can be broken down into allies, facilitators, and decoration. Enemies can be broken down into rivals, aggressive enemies, and passive enemies. This breakdown is only one of the many ways you can categorize characters within a game, but it is sufficient for this book.

Player Characters

A *player character* is controlled by a player. In many games there is only one player character—the one being controlled by the player. Some games, such as real-time strategy or team sports games, have the player control multiple characters.

The amount of control the player has over a character depends on the type of game that is being played. For example, a fighting game will give the player a lot of control over the character. The player can control the movement and actions of the character in detail. Adventure games are similar in that the player can control the character's actions to navigate through the world. Other games, such as real-time strategy games, give the player control over position, and the character intelligently acts upon environment and game events.

Multiplayer games feature several player-controlled characters in a single game. Some of these games are made up entirely of player-controlled characters. Many multiplayer games allow the player to customize his character—some go so far as to include a character editor with the game.

Character editors represent a particular problem for the concept artist. When a character editor is part of the game, the concept artist needs to create general character types that can be modified to achieve different looks. Rather than designing characters, the concept artist has to create clothing, accessories, hair, faces, and any number of character attributes that can be mixed and matched to show how the editor works. The character design process becomes much more complex.

Non-Player Characters

Technically, any character that is not player-controlled is a non-player character; however, it is useful to split enemies off into their own group, separate from the rest of the NPCs in a game. Enemies are distinct because players have to react very differently to them than they do to other characters in the game.

NPCs are usually not overtly hostile to the player. They might be indifferent or show very limited reaction to the player, but they are not generally hostile unless provoked. Of course, if an NPC is provoked, he then becomes an enemy rather than an NPC. Likewise, if the player pacifies an enemy, the enemy changes roles and becomes an NPC.

Some games are filled with NPCs. Team sports games, for example, feature NPCs that play the roles of teammates, cheerleaders, spectators, announcers, and so on. Although they might not necessarily try to kill the player character, the opposing team is better classified as an enemy because its goal is to defeat the player.

Probably the best examples of NPCs are found in adventure games. In an adventure game, the player interacts with several NPCs on many different levels. Some of the characters in the game might help the player by giving him information or items. Others might be indifferent, yet help in their own way, such as a store clerk or another type of merchant. Some characters might be nothing but decorative, giving no useful information and acting as a distraction.

In some games the NPCs change roles depending on the player's actions. For example, an indifferent merchant might change to an ally if the player completes a quest or helps solve a problem. He might become an enemy if the player tries to steal something from his shop.

When designing characters, the concept artist needs to understand what the character's role is and create a character who fits that role. A sleazy police informant should not wear a three-piece suit. A military guard should not be of a slight build. An opposing linebacker should not be obese. In other words, the character needs to fit the role.

Enemies

Enemies are non-player-controlled characters that try to keep the player from winning the game. The opposing team in a sports game is an enemy. The evil creatures in a horror game might be enemies. The other drivers in a racing game are enemies. The vicious alien trying to kill the player in a first-person shooter is an enemy.

In some games enemies are very intelligent and cunning, while in others they might simply be aggressive. In a football game, the opposing team might be very good at play calling and disguising play coverage. In a shooter, the enemies might be very good at ganging up on the player. In a fighting game, the enemy or opponent might have several combo moves. Each of these types of enemies is designed to challenge the player.

In designing enemies, the look of the character is often as important as what he does in the game. The characters should be intimidating to the player, causing him to feel a sense of accomplishment when he defeats the enemies. Sometimes the intimidation is due to an imposing physical appearance, but other times the intimidation is subtler, such as in a quiz game in which the opponent needs to appear intelligent.

Getting Ideas for Characters

One of the concept artist's toughest jobs is getting ideas for good characters. Designing a good character takes a lot of work. Sometimes the artist will go through dozens of sketches and still not have just the right character. Sometimes the artist needs help coming up with a great character design. So where can an artist look for inspiration for characters?

One of the best sources for inspiration for human characters is to observe your surroundings. Sometimes the best inspiration comes from normal day-to-day observance of people. A good practice is to go to a public place with a sketchbook in hand and draw. Figure 8.1 shows a sketchbook page dealing with everyday people in a public place. The sketches were done very quickly, with very little emphasis on detail. Most people don't hold a pose for very long, so the object is to get some quick general impressions.

hint

Some people become uncomfortable if they know someone is drawing them. If the drawing is recognizable as a specific person, you should always get permission from the person you are drawing. Unrecognizable quick sketches usually are not a problem. But a good way to avoid problems when drawing in a public place is to wear sunglasses, which prevent direct eye contact with people, making it less obvious who you are drawing.

Another great source for inspiration for characters is to look at other artists' work. There are many wonderful examples of characters in great masterpieces of art, comic books, movies, and other media. All of these media have great examples of character design. A good way to be the best is to learn from the best. Study how other artists deal with and solve the problems of designing a character.

Copying great masterpieces is a long-standing tradition in art that goes back to the Middle Ages. However, copying should be done only as a study and never as an original piece of artwork that you use for a commercial purpose.

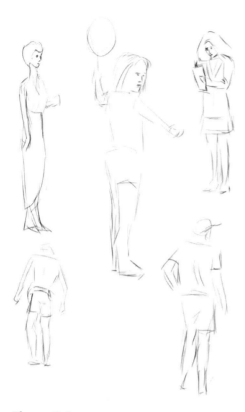

Figure 8.1
Quick character studies from everyday life

Drawing Characters

Drawing characters might be one of the most difficult tasks a concept artist has to face. The problem is compounded when the character is human. The issue with human characters is that everybody is familiar with the human form. If the artist moves a branch or two on a tree, for example, few people will notice; however, most people will recognize it if the artist moves a person's eye a fraction of an inch. Creating great human characters requires that the artist become very good at drawing the human figure.

This book will not attempt to give you a complete understanding of figure drawing. Figure drawing is a vast subject, and there are many good books and resources to help artists learn how to draw the figure. However, this book will show you some of the basics to help you get started.

Why Quick Sketches?

Quick sketches are used in game development for several reasons. In games in which many characters are needed but several are minor characters, the minor characters commonly will not receive the same treatment as the major characters. Rather than full renderings of these characters, a quick sketch is sufficient for the development process.

When you are developing major characters for games, the process usually includes a thumbnail stage in which idea drawings are created. From the idea drawings, three or four are chosen for further development into more developed quick sketches. Then, the final character is selected for a detailed rendering.

In some cases the main character needs to have more than one drawing to show different clothing or other changes to his appearance. In addition, more drawings might be needed to show how the character moves or animates during the game. Doing full renderings of the character for these drawings is unnecessary; quick sketches are usually all that are required.

Drawing the Head

A good way to think of the human head is to start with basic geometric shapes. First draw a circle. The problem with a circle is that it is flat. Draw a line around the circle to make it a sphere, as shown in Figure 8.2, so the circle is no longer flat and it looks more like a ball. The line should divide the sphere into two halves. It will be the guide for the center of the character's face.

The sphere will act as the main part of the head. The next step is to draw in the lower portion of the face and jaw line. Figure 8.3 shows how this is done.

Figure 8.2
Start to draw the head by creating a sphere.

Figure 8.3
Draw in the jaw line.

Now the basic shape of the head is completed. For the rest of the drawing, you will refine and define the features of the face and head. Start by drawing another line around the head in about the position of the eyebrows. This line will define the upper bridge of the nose.

Using the center line and the eyebrow line, construct a nose. Figure 8.4 shows the head with the nose, mouth, and cheekbone.

Now the building blocks are in place so you can add the detail of the face. Use the construction lines to draw in the eyes, mouth, ear, and other facial features, as shown in Figure 8.5.

Figure 8.4
Start the nose from the eyebrow line.

Figure 8.5
Define the facial features using the construction lines.

The construction lines help you draw the features of the face in their correct places. Continue drawing the face, adding lines for the hair and neck (see Figure 8.6).

Figure 8.6
Add more detail to the face.

When most of the features are drawn in, you can erase the construction lines, as shown in Figure 8.7. In this drawing the construction lines were drawn in heavily so they would reproduce well. Typically, you should draw the construction lines very lightly so they are easy to remove once the face is drawn.

Figure 8.7
Erase the construction lines.

In this drawing the head is looking down. Using the geometric construction method, you should be able to draw the head from any position. Drawing the head takes some practice. You should fill several pages with heads in different positions to get the feel of it.

Drawing the Full Figure

Drawing the figure is similar to drawing the head except that, while the head is pretty much a ball with features added, the figure is a flexible form with extreme movement possibilities. When drawing the figure, you need to interpret the dynamics of the range of motion within the character's pose. You also need to take into account the distribution of weight.

Standing characters should have an even distribution of their body weight. One leg can be carrying the majority of the weight, but to look correct it should be positioned under the character so the weight is balanced over that leg.

The first step in creating a figure is to define the natural position of the body with a few lines that define the relative placement of limbs and balance. Figure 8.8 shows the basic layout of the character. The lines look a little like a modified stick figure. The weight is on the back leg, so the leg is angled under the character to support him.

When drawing a figure, one of the biggest mistakes an artist might make is to commit to a specific line too early. It is better to draw multiple lines in an attempt to get a feeling for the figure. Draw the lines lightly and define the forms with pencil strokes. Figure 8.9 shows how the figure starts to emerge out of the many construction lines used in the drawing.

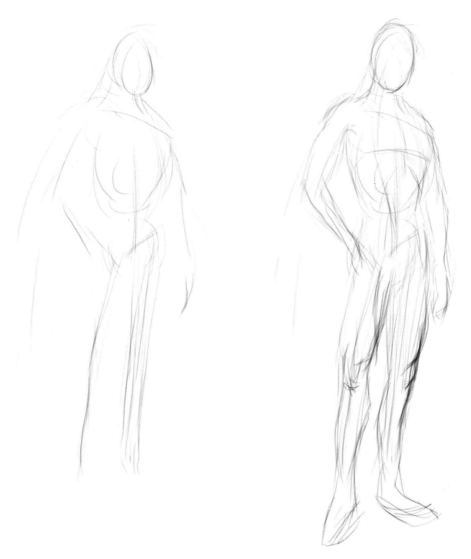

Figure 8.8
Use lines to define body positions and weight distribution.

Figure 8.9
Draw many lines to define the form of the body.

The same loose approach to defining the figure is also used to define the clothing and weapons the character is carrying (see Figure 8.10).

When the basic shapes are defined, you can use more definite lines to render the character. Figure 8.11 shows the stronger lines and shades starting to come out of the lighter construction lines. In some places the earlier lines need to be cleaned up to better show the new, more definite lines.

Figure 8.10
Continue to define the clothing and weapons.

Figure 8.11
Add more definite lines to the drawing.

The drawing really moves to more of a rendering mode as each form is defined. In Figure 8.12, the weapons are sketched in with heavier lines and some shading.

Sometimes the drawing might still need some changes, even after the initial heavier lines are drawn. In Figure 8.13, the shoulder has been changed to better express the natural folds of the character's clothing. In addition, some darker areas were added to the cape to bring out the character better.

Figure 8.12
The weapons are better defined.

Figure 8.13
Sometimes the drawing needs to be changed.

In the end, many of the original construction lines are left in the character sketch because they are not distracting from the drawing, and because the drawing is a quick sketch rather than a finished rendering of the character. Figure 8.14 shows the finished sketch.

Figure 8.14
All the construction lines are not removed from the finished sketch.

Character Exaggeration

Many games exaggerate the human figure to achieve a desired effect. For example, an enemy might be given large shoulders and arms to make him appear more menacing, or a female character might have longer legs to make her seem more athletic and appealing.

One of the most common forms of exaggeration is to give the character an abnormally large head. There are usually two reasons for exaggerating the head. The first reason is that larger heads tend to make the character more childlike or cute. Babies' heads are quite a bit larger in proportion to their bodies than adults' heads. The second reason for enlarging the head is that it is the focal point of the character. In many early games in which character resolution was a problem, the head was enlarged to give the character more detail.

Start the drawing by roughing in the basic shape of the character. Figure 8.15 shows the loose construction lines used to begin the sketch.

To enhance the feeling of a cute, innocent character, enlarge the character's eyes and oversize his clothing. Draw in the lines for the character as curves to avoid harsh angles. All of these elements give the character a softer, more childlike appearance.

Continue to define the character's features, as shown in Figure 8.16.

Figure 8.15
Draw in the basic construction lines for the character.

Figure 8.16
Develop the character's features.

When creating cute characters, you should use simple forms and avoid excessive detail. Draw in the remaining detail and clean up the sketch. Figure 8.17 shows the final sketch.

Figure 8.17
Finish the sketch by cleaning up the construction lines.

Non-Human Characters

Some characters in games are non-human. They might be animals, robots, aliens, imaginary or fantasy creatures, or almost anything the designer can imagine. Drawing these types of characters is both creative and challenging—creative because the artist can use a lot of imagination, and challenging because there are fewer structural guidelines.

hint

When you are drawing imaginary characters, it is a good practice to base the character on some form of reality. Make sure the joints work. The muscles should move the joints in the correct directions. The character should look like it could move and work in a normal environment, with the same gravitational effects as the rest of the characters in the game.

As always, the best way to start drawing a character is to do a few thumbnail sketches until you come up with something that looks good. Choose the best idea, and then rough it in with light construction lines, as shown in Figure 8.18.

Figure 8.18
Lightly draw the construction lines for the character.

This character is a magical creature from some ancient underground race. He is humanoid in that he walks semi-erect on two legs. His hands and feet are clawed, and his skin is knobby and leathery. His clothing is ceremonial, rather than used as a covering.

The beginning of the drawing should be free and flowing. Continue to define the creature. Figure 8.19 shows the drawing in progress.

The drawing is now beginning to take shape. Define the facial features and continue to work on the cloak and staff. The drawing should look like Figure 8.20.

Figure 8.19
Add more definition to the drawing.

Figure 8.20
Add facial features and detail to the staff.

As the drawing becomes more defined, the lines become more deliberate and less free-flowing. Figure 8.21 shows the character as he starts to come together as a more solid form. Notice the bumpy skin of his head and the shading of his cloak.

Now that the drawing is well defined in shape and form, you can add the detail and shading. Figure 8.22 shows the finished drawing. Because the construction lines were drawn in lightly, there is almost no cleanup necessary.

Figure 8.21
Start refining the forms in the drawing by adding detail and shading.

Figure 8.22
Continue to add detail and shading until the sketch is finished.

When it comes to imaginary characters, there is an infinite variety of possibilities. Sometimes the artist will come up with great ideas for characters by doing some experimental drawing, but the best way to approach the creation of an imaginary creature is to write a brief description of the character before sketching. At the beginning of this exercise, there was a written description of the character. This written description helped me create the character and keep him in line with the needs of the game.

Summary

Character creation is one of the most rewarding and challenging jobs for the concept artist. It is very rewarding for the artist to see a character that he designed in a game. It is also challenging to come up with characters that enhance the game design.

This chapter was devoted to character creation and drawing. You should now be familiar with many aspects of character creation. In this chapter, you should have learned the following concepts:

- What game characters are
- The differences between player characters, non-player characters, and enemies
- Where to find inspiration for creating characters
- How to draw characters
- The purpose of quick sketches in game design
- How to draw the head
- How to draw the figure
- How to exaggerate the figure
- How to create non-human characters

Questions

1. Why is character creation important in game design?
2. Who has the main responsibility for creating interesting characters?
3. What are game characters?
4. What is the software that controls game characters called?
5. What is a character that is controlled by the player called?
6. What does NPC stand for?
7. What is the object of an enemy character?
8. For the concept artist, what purpose does observing people in day-to-day life serve?
9. Should the artist look at the work of other character designers?
10. How do basic geometric shapes help the artist construct the head?
11. Why should construction lines be kept free and flowing?
12. What does distribution of weight mean in a character drawing?

13. What do the few light beginning lines of the position of the limbs and body balanced over the feet define?

14. What is one way the artist can achieve a childlike or cute look for a character?

15. Should the artist be concerned with proper movement for a fantasy creature?

Answers

1. Because the characters are the focal point of the game.

2. The concept artist.

3. All intelligent people or creatures in a game.

4. Artificial intelligence.

5. A player character.

6. Non-player character.

7. To defeat the player.

8. It provides inspiration for character designs.

9. Yes.

10. They help make the head three-dimensional, and they help the artist place the features correctly.

11. So the artist does not commit to a line too early in the drawing process.

12. The character should look balanced.

13. The natural position of the body.

14. By enlarging the head.

15. Yes.

Discussion Questions

1. Why is the study of figure drawing important in character design?

2. What should an artist consider when designing an enemy?

3. Why are characters so important in game design?

4. What effect does exaggeration of the head have on a character?

5. What is the future of character design?

Exercises

1. Create a sketch of a main character for a futuristic police game. Make the character pleasant but strong, without him being overbearing.

2. Create a heroine character for a horror adventure game. Make her appealing without being overtly sexy. Give her a sense of innocence combined with strength.

3. Create a truly terrifying enemy character for a military game. He should be the final character in the game, and he should make the player think twice before attacking.

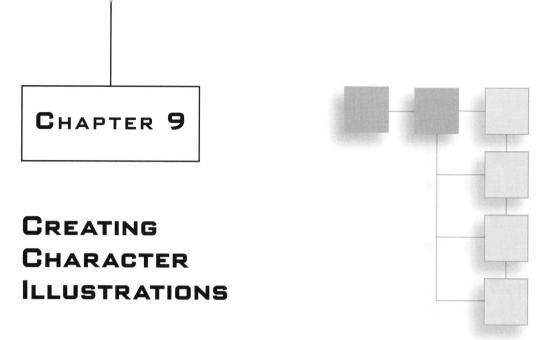

CHAPTER 9

CREATING CHARACTER ILLUSTRATIONS

Character sketches are great, but they don't give the development team any information about colors. They also don't contain enough detail for the development team to accurately create the character. For that, a more detailed full-color illustration is needed.

This chapter is about creating full-color character illustrations. It will cover what character illustrations are and how they are used in games. It will also give you some tips for creating good character illustrations, as well as examples of creating a simple color character illustration and a more detailed character illustration.

This chapter is a continuation from the last chapter and will build upon some of the concepts covered in that chapter.

Character Illustrations

A *character illustration* is a full-color, detailed painting of a character. It can be done in almost any color medium that the artist prefers, as long as there is sufficient detail for the design team to use the illustration to create the character for the game. The character illustration is similar to the environment illustration in that it does not have to be absolutely accurate, but it does have to have a higher level of accuracy than the environment illustration. A character illustration is used more directly by the development team in creating game art than an environment illustration is.

Character illustrations are works of art that focus on a single character to define not only the look of the character, but his disposition and nature as well. When creating a character illustration, the artist must take into account the character's personality. If the character is a small, cute mouse, the illustration should convey that concept. If the character is a large enemy alien, the illustration should be very different from the mouse illustration. Part of the character illustration's purpose is to help the design team understand the type of character they are creating. If the character illustration can convey the message of the character's personality, the chance of the development artists' success increases dramatically.

Character templates will be introduced in the following chapter. A *character template* is a scale drawing of a character for use in building the character model. A character illustration is not used as a template for creating a 3D model; rather, it is used as reference for creating the model.

How Are Character Illustrations Used?

A character illustration is a multipurpose work of art. It is primarily used to communicate to the development team information about the character, but it has many other purposes as well, including inspiration, promotion, and funding.

The primary purpose of a character illustration is to give information. The development team uses the character illustration for reference when creating the game artwork and animations for the character.

The character illustration is also used as inspiration, similar to the environment illustration. Developing characters for games is an interpretive process. Game characters move and react to events in the game. As technology has advanced, the complexity of the game character personality has expanded. The character illustration is a snapshot into the personality of the character. It should inspire the development team to create and animate the character.

Many character illustrations are used to promote the game. Often a character illustration is used in the advertising or promotional material because it is usually the first finished piece of artwork available.

The character illustration is one of the first things a review committee might look at when determining the funding for a game. The characters in a game have a profound impact on a publisher's acceptance of the game for publication. Having very good character illustrations in the game design can be a plus for getting the game funded, while poor character illustrations can stop the funding very quickly.

Character illustrations also are often used as the basis for creating templates for the model construction of the character.

What Makes a Good Character Illustration?

It takes many things to create a good character illustration. The first and most important aspect of a good character illustration is that the illustration should capture the look and personality of the character. There needs to be enough detail for the development team to see how to build the character and any clothing or accessories that he might be wearing or carrying. It should also indicate how the clothing might move about the character or how the character might move. If the character is an old man with a cane who moves very slowly, the character illustration needs to show the old man bent over the cane, obviously having trouble moving.

Because character illustrations are often used for promotion or funding of the game, they need to be well designed and clear to the viewer. The artist should take some time to plan the character illustration so it demonstrates good composition.

Ambiguity in a character illustration is not usually a good idea. If the illustration does not show the detail of the character clearly, it can cause misinterpretations when the character is built for the game. A good character illustration also should not use harsh lighting that obscures parts of the character.

A good character illustration should have correct anatomy. Many problems in building a character can be avoided if the character's proportions are drawn correctly. Most characters in games are 3D, so if a character is out of proportion or the limbs are not reasonable for movement in the game world, it can create many problems for the development team.

One of the basic components of a character illustration is that it is in color. Often the character illustration is used as the color reference for the development team because character templates don't always have color, and character sketches also aren't in color. A good character illustration needs to have the correct colors for the character.

Simple Character Illustrations

Not all character illustrations need to be finished to the same level of detail. Most character illustrations are detailed color sketches only used in the design document for the development team. If there are no outside purposes for the illustration, the level of detail does not need to be as high.

This example of a simple character illustration will show you how the majority of character illustrations are created. Later in the chapter, I'll give you a more elaborate example.

The first step in creating a character illustration is to start with a good character sketch. Figure 9.1 shows the base drawing for a female ranger in a fantasy game. The drawing should be detailed but not shaded; the shading will be applied in the painting.

The media for this painting are airbrush and hand-painting. The airbrush is used to lay in a simple background for the illustration. The background colors are applied to the entire surface of the drawing. As the painting progresses, the background colors in the character will help unify the colors of the painting. Figure 9.2 shows the first pass of color applied to the painting (although it is difficult to see in a black-and-white book!).

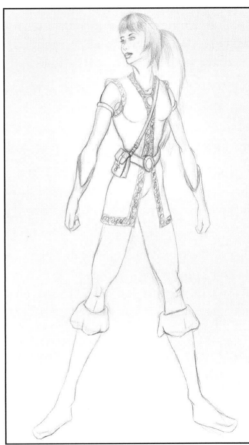

Figure 9.1
Start with a drawing of the character.

Figure 9.2
Add the background color to the painting.

In Figure 9.3, the background is enhanced with darker colors around the edges of the painting and a lighter color directly behind the character. The design principle here is to focus the attention toward the center of the painting. The lighter background color will be contrasted with the darker colors used in the character. Figure 9.3 also shows the beginning of the flesh tones added to the painting.

When using an airbrush, you move from one area of the painting to the next. The areas that are not being painted are masked off so you can apply paint only to the appropriate areas. In Figure 9.3, the face and arms were left uncovered while the rest of the painting was masked.

In Figure 9.4, the lighter pinks of the flesh are added. The mask remains the same, but the colors airbrushed over the area change. (Again, this is difficult to see in the book; however, you can check out the full-color illustration on the book's CD-ROM.)

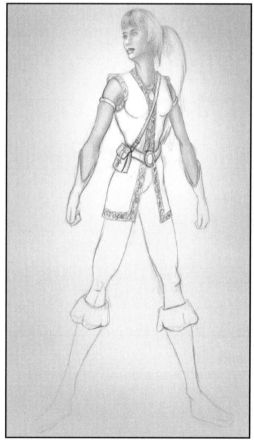

Figure 9.3
Use the background to highlight the character.

Figure 9.4
Paint the colors of the skin.

The next mask will isolate the character's hair. The character will have blond hair, so the basic shades of light to dark are applied with the airbrush (see Figure 9.5).

The airbrush does not do a very good job on individual strands of hair. To get a good representation of hair, use a small brush to apply the darker and lighter areas by hand. Figure 9.6 shows the progress of the hair. (Again, the full-color images on the CD-ROM will better demonstrate this.)

 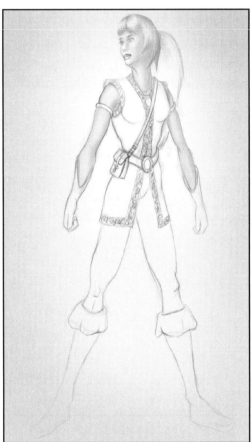

Figure 9.5
Mask around the hair and airbrush the basic colors.

Figure 9.6
Paint the dark and light areas of the hair by hand.

The character has a long ponytail, which is also painted in using the same technique as the hair on the top of her head (see Figure 9.7).

After the hair, the next area to paint is the character's tunic. This area is masked off, and the airbrush is used to paint the darker areas, and then the lighter ones (refer to Figure 9.7).

The borders of the tunic have some golden embroidery. Just like with the hair, the airbrush does not do a very good job of creating the embroidery. The base darker color is painted in with the airbrush, and the finer detail is then painted in by hand. Figure 9.8 shows the results.

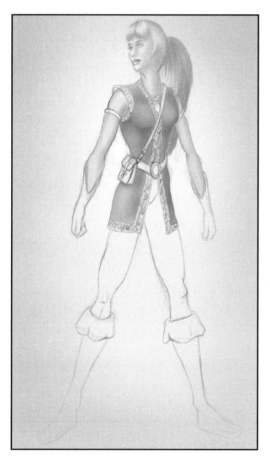
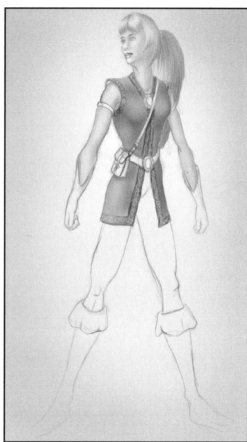

Figure 9.7
Paint the ponytail and the tunic.

Figure 9.8
Paint in the finer detail of the embroidery by hand.

Several other items need to be painted by hand because of their size or detail. Figure 9.9 shows the addition of these areas. The facial features are painted in, as well as some of the arm jewelry. The pouch strap and collar brooch are also painted by hand.

The only elements that remain to finish the upper body of the character are the pouch belt and gloves. These are painted in the same way as the other elements, with the airbrush laying in the base darker colors and the finer detail painted by hand (see Figure 9.10).

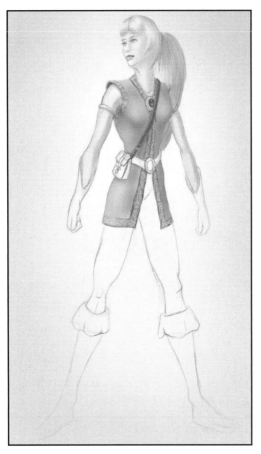

Figure 9.9
Paint some of the smaller items by hand.

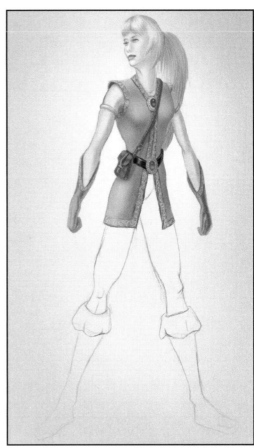

Figure 9.10
Paint the gloves, belt, and pouch to finish the upper portion of the character.

Next the legs are masked off and painted using the airbrush. There is little detail in the character's leggings, so they are completed with just the use of the airbrush (see Figure 9.11).

The last step to finish the character is to airbrush in her boots and clean up some of the pencil lines that are still showing. You can remove the pencil lines using an opaque paint that is the same color as the background. Figure 9.12 shows the finished character illustration.

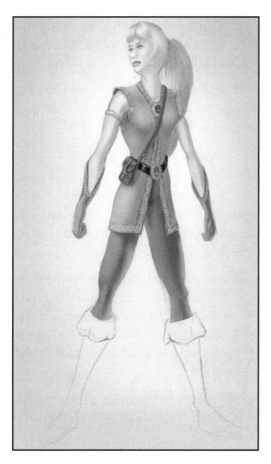

Figure 9.11
Next, airbrush in the legs of the character.

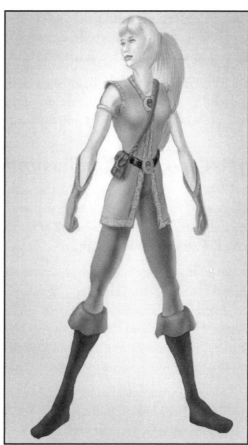

Figure 9.12
Finish the illustration by cleaning up the remaining pencil lines.

Notice that the contrast of the background brings out the character as the focal point of the picture. There is greater detail in the upper part of the body, so the focus is on that area. The subtle touch is that the character's lips are red. They are the only really red part of the picture. The illustration is made up of mostly a blue/yellow scheme, so the use of red on the character's mouth draws the eye to that area. Check out the image on the CD-ROM to see what I mean.

The character shows confidence and strength by her stance, with her legs braced apart and her arms at a ready position. Her jewelry shows her to be a woman of substance, as does her embroidered tunic. She has an athletic, elongated build.

This illustration is not a full, finished character illustration. With a little more planning and a lot more detail, the illustration could become a full, finished illustration. The next example will show you how a full, finished illustration is planned and completed.

Detailed Character Illustrations

A detailed, finished character illustration takes more planning and time to create than a simple character illustration. In many ways, the detailed, finished character illustration is the closest thing to a finished work of art that a concept artist creates. In fact, many character illustrations of this nature could adorn the walls of a gallery.

When approaching the detailed character illustration, the artist already should have gone through the process of creating a character sketch. Because of the time involved in creating a detailed illustration, the artist might have several sketches and thumbnails of the character. There should be quite a bit of refinement of the character before the work starts on the illustration. It would be sad to finish a detailed character illustration only to find out that there was a major problem with the character.

The following example is a character illustration in oil paint on a panel. The color medium is unimportant, but oil paint has the advantage of not drying quickly, which allows the artist to blend colors on the surface of the painting.

The first task is to rough in the basic forms of the character on the panel. Figure 9.13 shows the initial construction lines of the drawing.

A detailed line drawing is then created. The line drawing does not have any shading because its purpose is to guide the painting. The shading will be added later. Figure 9.14 shows the base line drawing.

This character is your run-of-the-mill knight on chicken back. The circle behind the knight is a design element to help keep the focus on the character.

Figure 9.13
Rough in the basic construction lines of the drawing.

Figure 9.14
Create a detailed line drawing of the character.

Before you go to the trouble of starting to apply paint to the panel, it is a good idea to work out the color scheme of the painting. You can create a small color painting with the basic color and value information. This small painting will then be the guide for painting the illustration. Figure 9.15 shows the small color rendering.

Figure 9.15
A small color rendering helps you plan the colors and values of the illustration.

In the first example in this chapter, you used a mask to shield the painting. In this example, a mask is used to protect the character from the background. The mask will protect the area where the character will later be painted. That way, you can paint the background without having to work around the character. Figure 9.16 shows the background painted over the top of the character.

After the background is painted the mask is removed, revealing the drawing of the character. The drawing can then be used as a guide for painting the character. Figure 9.17 shows the mask removed from the painting.

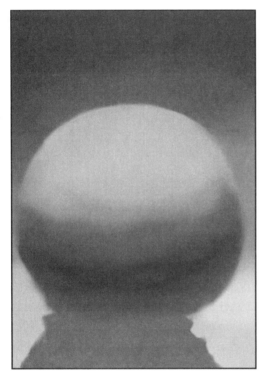

Figure 9.16
The background is painted over the character.

Figure 9.17
Remove the mask from the painting.

Using the small color scheme as a guide, paint the base colors in flat tones. Figure 9.18 shows the head of the chicken roughed in using color. The drawing is used as a guide for applying the tones.

The rest of the knight and chicken is painted in flat tones, like the head shown in Figure 9.18. The entire painting should now have paint on it. The advantage of painting in all the tones before moving on to painting detail in any area is that the artist is able to see whether the basic composition and values of the painting work. At this stage of the painting, it is easier to change something wrong than it is to change it later, when a lot of work has gone into it. Figure 9.19 shows the painting in flat tones.

Figure 9.18
The head of the chicken is painted in flat tones.

Figure 9.19
Cover the entire panel with the base flat tones.

Now that the flat tones of the painting are down, you can begin the detail work. Starting at the bottom of the painting, paint the rocks next because the chicken will stand on top of them and it is easier to paint them and then paint the chicken's feet on top of them. Figure 9.20 shows the rocks with the beginning of the chicken's feet on top of them. Also, paint the knight's lance behind the chicken's head.

Next, paint the knight, who is encased in armor. The armor is decorated with etched metal. To achieve the look of etched metal, paint the basic colors and values of the armor, and then apply the etching in a darker color using a fine brush. See Figure 9.21 for the results of the work.

Figure 9.20
The rocks are brought to life beneath the chicken.

Figure 9.21
Paint the knight next.

Following the same procedure as you used for the knight's armor, paint the chicken's barding, as shown in Figure 9.22.

When you are working on the chicken's feathers, the nice aspect of painting in oils is that you can brush the lighter white paint into the darker gray paint. You can then paint the feathers relatively quickly and with good effect. Figure 9.23 shows the detailed work around the chicken's head. Some orange is added to a few of the feathers to tie them into the environment.

Figure 9.22
Paint the barding using the same technique you used for the armor.

Figure 9.23
Paint the detail of the chicken's head.

Working from left to right, paint the lower feathers and legs of the chicken (see Figure 9.24).

Now the only thing left is to paint the tail feathers. Like you did for the other feathers, add yellow and orange to tie the character in to the environment. Figure 9.25 shows the finished character illustration.

Figure 9.24
Continue to paint the chicken, working on the lower body and legs.

Figure 9.25
Finish the illustration by painting in the tail feathers.

Summary

The last two chapters covered many aspects of character sketches and illustrations. This chapter dealt with character illustrations. A character illustration is a detailed, full-color painting of the character. The illustration should be well designed and well rendered because it is not only used for design information, but also for promotion and funding of the game. The character illustration is usually the most refined and finished piece of artwork in the game design.

In this chapter, you should have learned the following concepts:

- The difference between a character illustration and a sketch
- The definition of a character illustration
- How character illustrations are used in game designs
- What makes a good character illustration
- How to create a simple character illustration
- How to create a detailed, finished character illustration

Questions

1. What is the difference between a character sketch and a character illustration?
2. Must a character illustration have greater accuracy than an environment illustration?
3. Should a character illustration convey the character's personality?
4. Are character illustrations generally used as templates for creating 3D characters?
5. Other than to provide information for the development team, what other uses are there for character illustrations?
6. Why are character illustrations used in promotional and advertising material for games?
7. What is the most important aspect of a good character illustration?
8. Why is ambiguity usually not a good idea for character illustrations?
9. Why are colors in a character illustration so important?
10. True or false: All character illustrations need to be finished to the same level of detail.
11. How are character drawings used to create character illustrations?
12. Should character drawings used to create character illustrations be shaded?
13. Why is an airbrush a poor choice for painting strands of hair?
14. Why should an artist take more time to plan a detailed character illustration than other concept art?
15. What advantage does oil paint have over many other types of color media?

Answers

1. Character illustrations are detailed, full-color paintings, and character sketches are usually drawings.
2. Yes.
3. Yes.

4. No.

5. Inspiration, promotion, and funding.

6. Because they are usually the most finished artwork in the design.

7. That it capture the look and personality of the character.

8. Because ambiguity might cause misinterpretations when the character is created.

9. The character illustration is often the only color reference the design team will have when creating the character.

10. False.

11. They form the guidelines for the concept artist to add the color to the painting.

12. No.

13. Because an airbrush is not very effective for painting fine detail.

14. Because the character illustration is often the most finished piece of artwork the artist will create.

15. Oil paints allow the artist to blend colors on the picture.

Discussion Questions

1. What uses can character illustrations have?

2. Why are character illustrations more finished than other concept art?

3. What are the characteristics of a good character illustration?

4. Why are good character proportions important in character illustrations?

5. Why is it important to plan a detailed character illustration?

Exercises

1. Create a simple character illustration of a young child for a kids' sports game. Make the child athletic yet cute.

2. Create a simple color illustration of a character for a military game. The character should look strong and carry some kind of menacing weapon.

3. Create a detailed character illustration of a character for a street skateboarding game. The character should have a modern look and fit into an urban environment.

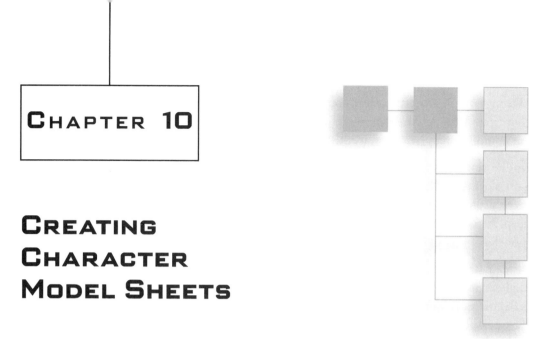

CHAPTER 10

CREATING CHARACTER MODEL SHEETS

C haracter illustrations are great for all the reasons mentioned in the Chapter 9, but they alone are not enough to complete a game design document. Another critical piece of artwork for the concept artist to create is the model sheet. This chapter is about creating model sheets. It will cover what model sheets are and how they are used in game development. It will also cover creating base templates for male and female characters. Then, you will learn how a model sheet is created using a base template.

What Are Model Sheets?

A *model sheet* is a template created by the concept artist to help the development team create accurate models of the designed characters. The model sheet is an orthographic rendering of the character drawn from different views. Each view is designed to give the development team vital information about the character.

Many characters in games today are very detailed. Games are getting closer and closer to reality in their graphics. Things that were impossible only a few years ago, such as cloth movement, facial animation, specular lighting, bump mapping, and transparency, are commonplace today. The movement to realism in characters is putting a lot of pressure on concept artists and development teams to create better characters. The model sheet is the vital link between the concept artist and the development team.

Model sheets are a form of art borrowed from the motion picture animation industry. When animators started drawing characters, they had to keep the character looking consistent in all the scenes. Back then, all the frames of animation were drawn by hand. The problem became even more daunting when multiple artists worked on the same character. To help solve the problem, the industry came up with a system to help the animators keep their drawings consistent. The model sheet was a big part of that system.

Another industry where model sheets are used extensively is the comic book industry. Like motion picture animation, comic animation has several artists working on the same character. Although the requirements for consistency are not as rigorous in comics as they are in motion pictures, they are still fairly rigid.

Unlike motion pictures and comics, games do not have as much hand-drawn art. Instead, games primarily use 3D models. The advantage of using a 3D model is that the character is consistent because the same model is used throughout the game. However, the need to keep the game character consistent with the designed character is still important. The model sheet helps address that need.

In many ways, model sheets are similar to drafting. The character is seen from different angles in isometric views. *Isometric* means without perspective. So in other words, the view is flat to the viewer, with no distortion for distance. Isometric drawings are more accurate than perspective drawings because the elements can be plotted directly from view to view. To see how this is done, start with a simple drawing of the head, as shown in Figure 10.1.

Figure 10.1
Start with a drawing of a head.

Next, draw the side view of the head to the right of the current drawing. Use lines from the original drawing to help you draw the features in the proper places. See Figure 10.2 for an example.

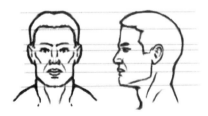

Figure 10.2
Project the side view of the head to the right of the original drawing.

The light-blue lines help you line up the features so both drawings are accurate. It is important to be accurate when you are drawing model sheets because the drawings are used as templates to create 3D models.

Next, create a side view above the side view you just drew, but rotate this new one 90 degrees counterclockwise, as shown in Figure 10.3. Draw in the guidelines, and then draw the top of the head.

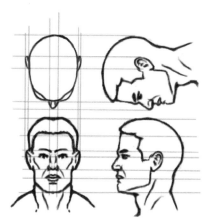

Figure 10.3
Draw a rotated side view and the top of the head.

The finished drawing is an orthogonal view of the head. *Orthogonal* means that the subject of the drawing is seen from multiple angles. Each angle shows a different view of the character, and the combination should provide enough information for a model builder to create the character.

How Are Model Sheets Used?

Model sheets are used for both reference and templates in creating 3D models. The problem with character illustrations for reference is that the illustration only shows the character from one direction, typically the front. What does the back of the character look like? To accurately create a game character, the development team needs to know what the character looks like from all angles.

Some model sheets are in color and some are line drawings. Figure 10.4 shows a model sheet of an earth elemental with color added to it to show how his skin will be different from a normal character.

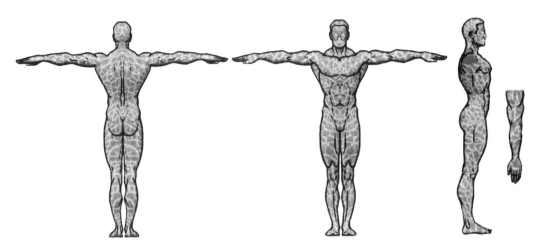

Figure 10.4
Some model sheets are in color.

Most model sheets are black-and-white line drawings because they tend to work better as templates when the team is developing the character. A *template* is a guide used to create 3D models. Figure 10.5 shows a model sheet used as a template in a 3D program.

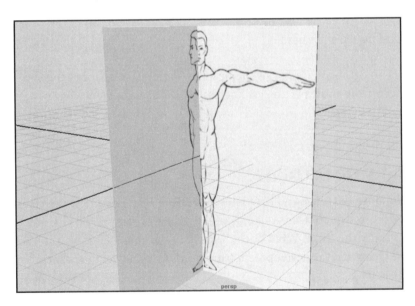

Figure 10.5
Model sheets are used as templates to create 3D models.

Notice that the model sheets intersect each other in the 3D program. This is why it is critical that the model sheet is accurate. When the 3D artist sets up the model sheets to create a model, some very undesirable results can occur in the modeling process if the drawings are not accurate.

The 3D artist uses the model sheets to construct the model. Figure 10.6 shows a 3D model of the torso as it is being built, using model sheets as a guide.

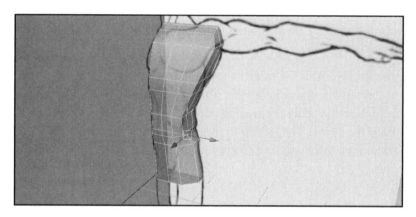

Figure 10.6
The torso is being built with the use of model sheets.

It is helpful for the concept artist to understand how the development team will use the concept art. If the purpose of the drawing is for reference, accuracy is not as critical as it is when the drawing is used directly in the development of the game art.

In addition to helping the development team create the characters for the game, model sheets are also good because they force the concept artist to fully design characters. Character illustrations do not contain detail from all angles, and therefore the artist doesn't fully design characters. Because creating a model sheet requires the artist to draw the character from several different perspectives, it forces the artist to fully design the character. Character designs are not typically complete without the model sheets.

Creating Base Model Sheets

Human characters are the most common type of character found in video games. A good place to start when you are creating model sheets is to develop base human characters with the proportions most commonly used in games. You can later use these base characters to create other characters without having to start from a plain white sheet of paper every time. These base characters become similar to mannequins in a clothing store; all the artist needs to do is dress them in different clothing to create different characters.

The Male Character

The human male character is very common in games. He is usually a powerfully built character with well-defined muscles. He can easily carry a 200-pound gun in one hand. Figure 10.7 shows the front view of a base male character.

The character should be drawn with the arms extended. They don't have to be straight out, as in Figure 10.7, but they do need to be out from the body. When an artist skins a 3D model (in other words, attaches the model to a set of bones for animation), the arms need to be out away from the body in many 3D programs. That is why you see most 3D models with their arms straight out to the sides.

A simple way to create the back view of the model sheet is to use a sheet of tracing paper. Because the drawings are orthogonal and isometric, the front and back views will have exactly the same outside proportions. Lay the tracing paper over the drawing of the front view and trace the outline of the figure. Then, draw in the surface detail for the back. Figure 10.8 shows the back view laid over the top of the front view.

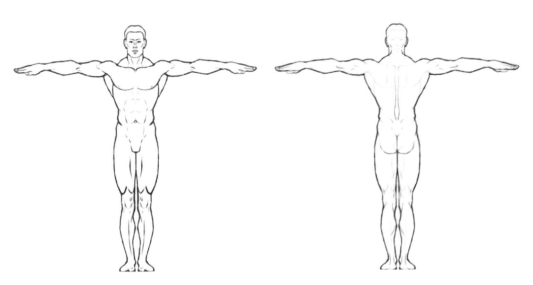

Figure 10.7
Draw the character from the front.

Figure 10.8
Lay the back view over the front view.

The side view is a little trickier. Take the front view and extend guidelines from the major features to the side. Use the guidelines to draw the side view, as shown in Figure 10.9.

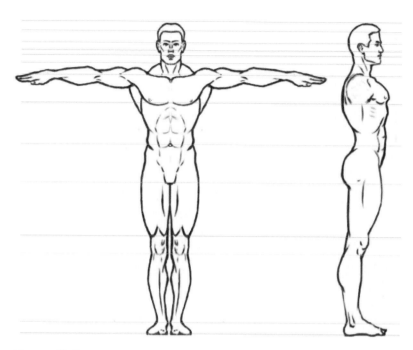

Figure 10.9
Use the guidelines to draw the side view.

The development team can usually get all the information they need to create the figure from the back, front, and side views, with the exception of the arms. The arms need a top view to help show depth, similar to how the body needs a side view. Draw the top view of the arm by extending lines from the front view upward, as shown in Figure 10.10.

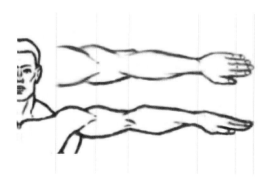

Figure 10.10
Extend guidelines upward to draw the top view
of the arm.

Now the base model sheets for the male character should be complete. Figure 10.11 shows the completed model sheet of the base male character.

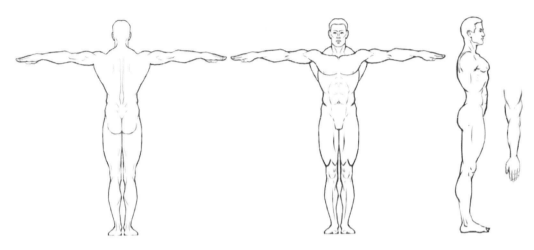

Figure 10.11
Each drawing should be proportional for the base male character.

The base model is a guide for creating characters with the same or similar proportions. It is not a good base for exaggerated characters. It is often a good idea to create a number of base model sheets for different body types.

The Female Character

Female game characters generally are more slender than male characters. Like the male characters, they are idealized in most cases. In fact, some are impossibly idealized. Female characters tend to be just as strong as male characters; however, their muscle definition usually is not as pronounced. Like the male character, a female character can carry a 200-pound gun easily in one hand. Even though in games a female character is powerful, she also is designed to be beautiful, so typically she does not have the same bulging muscles that a male character has.

The base female character is developed the same way as the base male character. Start with the front view. Figure 10.12 shows a front view of a base female character.

Notice that the female character is more slender than the male character. She is also drawn with her feet pointed slightly downward. This is because most female characters in games wear heels. By superimposing the female character over the male character, the differences between the two become very evident (see Figure 10.13).

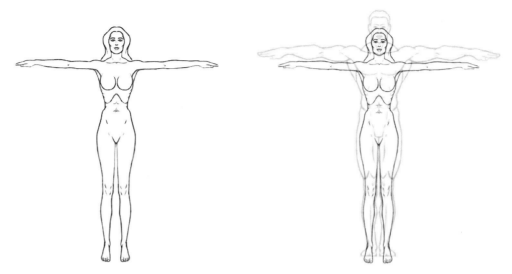

Figure 10.12
Start the model sheet by drawing a front view.

Figure 10.13
When the female character is superimposed over the male character, the differences become evident.

The female character model sheet is developed using the same steps as for the male character. Figure 10.14 shows the completed female character base model sheet.

Figure 10.14
The base model sheet for the female character is developed the same way as the male character's base model sheet.

Most female characters have long hair. This creates a problem when you are creating a model because the hair can obscure some areas of the character. To avoid this problem, it is always a good idea to draw the hair as transparent in the model sheet so the modeler can see all areas of the character.

Not all characters are human characters. Often a character is so unique that it doesn't make sense to create a base drawing for it. Instead, the concept artist simply creates the character as a model sheet from the beginning. However, having a variety of base model sheets is a great timesaver when you are working on new characters. It is a good idea to create base characters for several different body types. Even if a character isn't exactly the same as one of the body types, it is helpful to have something to start with and adapt it to the needs of the new character.

Creating the Template

To make an effective template for building 3D models, each view of the character in the model sheets must be proportional in the 3D program. Each view will be projected onto either a picture plane or a polygon in the 3D program. To make sure the 3D artist can import the model sheets accurately, the concept artist needs to create templates for each view at exactly the same dimensions. Figure 10.15 shows the model sheets converted to modeling templates.

Figure 10.15
Model sheets are converted into templates for 3D modeling.

Notice that each drawing is centered in the frame. This is vital so that the modeler is able to line up the drawings correctly. The modeler usually creates templates from the model sheets, but sometimes the concept artist is asked to create them. It is a good idea for the concept artist to understand how to make templates so he has a good idea of the importance of making sure every drawing is consistent.

Making Character Model Sheets

Creating character model sheets from a base model is an easy process. By laying a piece of tracing paper over the top of the base model, the artist can create the new character using parts of the base model as a guide. Figure 10.16 shows a warrior character laid over the base model.

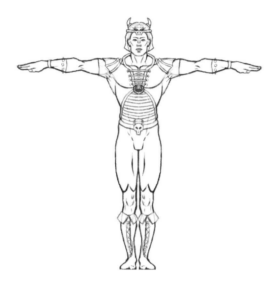

Figure 10.16
The warrior is developed from the base male model sheet.

The advantage of using the base model sheet is that if characters from that base model sheet have worked well in the past for animation, it is likely that new characters will work well too. Figure 10.17 shows the finished front drawing of the warrior character.

As shown earlier, you can use the front model sheet to create the rear view of the character. You use a sheet of tracing paper to create the back view of the character from the front drawing. Figure 10.18 shows the back view over the front view.

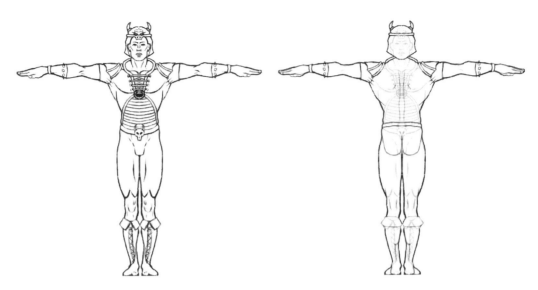

Figure 10.17
The finished warrior character in the front view

Figure 10.18
Create the back view using the front view as a guide.

When you have finished the front and back views, create lines across the paper to line up the back view with the front view and to draw the side view. Figure 10.19 shows the three views together.

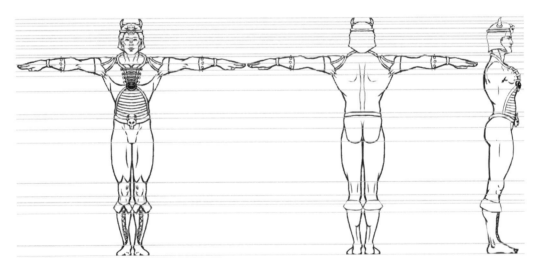

Figure 10.19
Use the guidelines to draw the side view.

To draw the arm correctly, you need to project upward from one of the character's arms, as shown in Figure 10.20.

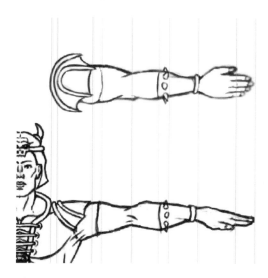

Figure 10.20
Draw the arm by projecting upward.

Now the model sheet of the warrior is complete. Each drawing of the character is accurate. Figure 10.21 shows the finished model sheet without the blue guidelines.

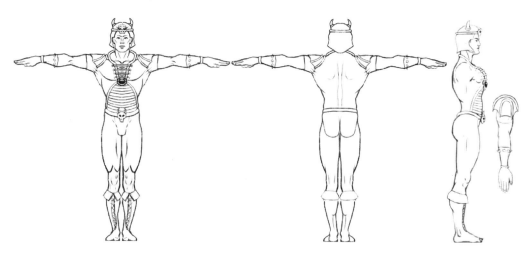

Figure 10.21
Removing the guidelines finishes the model sheet.

This character is symmetrical. Some characters will have differences from one side to the other. If this is the case, you will need to create an extra side view to show the differences from one side to the other. In all circumstances in which a character looks different from one side to another, you should create new views.

Color in Model Sheets

Sometimes a model sheet needs to be in color. This happens when very specific colors are needed for the character. Color in model sheets has the same purpose as any other aspect of the drawings: It gives more direction to the development team. Figure 10.22 shows an example of a full-color model sheet.

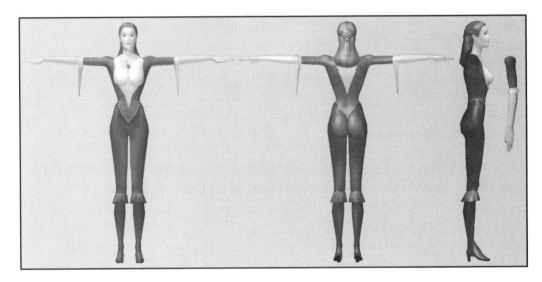

Figure 10.22
Some model sheets need to be in full color.

Full-color drawings for model sheets are obviously more expensive and take longer to create than line drawings. They are not created very often because usually the development team can pull the color information from the character illustration.

The issues regarding accuracy in full-color model sheets are the same as in black-and-white model sheets. The concept artist must be careful not to move detail around in the painting process when he is developing a full-color model sheet.

Model sheets don't always have to be of characters; sometimes models sheets are created for other game elements. Figure 10.23 shows a model sheet of a house.

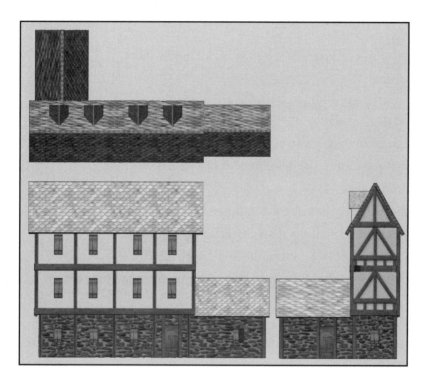

Figure 10.23
Model sheets can be for other objects in games as well.

Summary

This chapter covered several concepts regarding the creation and use of model sheets in game development. The use of model sheets in game development was borrowed from the animated motion picture industry, where the need for consistency in characters is critical. In games, model sheets are used as guides for the development team to create 3D models of characters.

In this chapter, you should have learned the following concepts:

- What model sheets are
- How model sheets are used in game development
- Why models sheets need to be accurate
- How to create a male base model sheet
- How to create a female base model sheet
- How to create a character model sheet
- How to create a model template

Questions

1. From where did the game industry borrow the use of model sheets?
2. What is a model sheet?
3. What type of art is used to keep the game characters consistent with the designed characters?
4. What is a drawing without perspective called?
5. What are guidelines used for in the development of a model sheet?
6. What is an orthogonal view?
7. Why are model sheets better than character illustrations for creating 3D models?
8. Why are model sheets more accurate than character illustrations?
9. Why are most model sheets black-and-white line drawings?
10. Why does the creation of model sheets help the concept artist more fully design a character?
11. What are base character model sheets?
12. Why are characters in model sheets drawn with their arms extended to their sides?
13. How should the drawings in a model template be positioned on a frame?
14. Why is it good for concept artists to understand how model templates are made?
15. Are model sheets only used for characters?

Answers

1. The motion picture animation industry.
2. A template created by the concept artist to help the development team create accurate models of the designed characters.
3. Model sheets.
4. An isometric drawing.
5. To help the artist transfer detail and proportions from one view to another.
6. A view that shows multiple perspectives of an object or character.
7. A character illustration only shows one side of the character.
8. Everything in a model sheet is plotted and sized correctly.
9. Line drawings tend to work better as model templates.
10. A model sheet forces the concept artist to design all sides of the character.
11. Model sheets of characters with the proportions most commonly used in games.
12. Because of skinning issues in 3D programs.

13. Centered.

14. So they understand how model sheets are used in game development.

15. No.

Discussion Questions

1. How are model sheets used in different industries?

2. What are the advantages of model sheets over character illustrations when you are creating 3D models?

3. What are some good reasons for creating base character model sheets?

4. Why is it a good idea for the concept artist to understand how model sheets are used in game development?

5. Why is accuracy so important in creating model sheets?

Exercises

1. Create a model sheet of a character from your favorite game. The model sheet should have enough views to take into account any differences from one side of the character to another.

2. Create a model sheet of a character you created in Chapter 8 or 9.

3. Create a model template from a model sheet you have created.

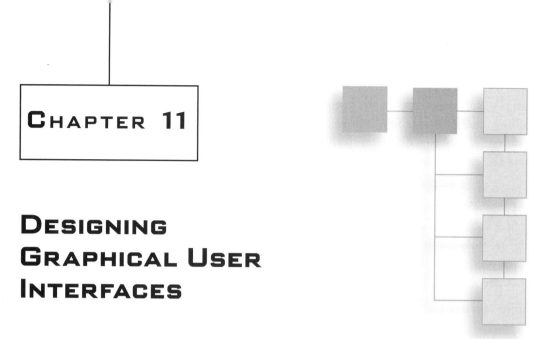

CHAPTER 11

DESIGNING GRAPHICAL USER INTERFACES

Games are interactive products, and they require some means for the user to control them. In games, the onscreen elements used to control the game are called the *graphical user interface* (or *GUI*, for short). This chapter will cover the basics of how GUIs are designed and the concept artist's role in creating GUI designs. It will cover what graphical user interfaces are, including some different types of graphical user interfaces. It will also give you examples of creating a menu design and onscreen elements.

From reading this chapter and working through some of the examples, you should gain a good understanding of the issues surrounding GUI design in games.

What Are Graphical User Interfaces?

Graphical user interfaces are any and all art used in a game for the purposes of player navigation or disseminating game information. That definition covers a lot of area, from onscreen displays to menus to credit screens. In some games, there is as much art in the GUI as there is in the rest of the game.

The amount of art required for the GUI in any particular game varies depending on the type of game and the amount of information and navigation issues involved. A simple online puzzle game might have only a title screen and some onscreen game controls. On the other hand, a flight simulator might have extensive navigation and information systems.

Information Screens

An information screen gives the player specific game information. A title screen is an information screen. Almost all games have a legal screen, which lets the player know who owns the copyrights and trademarks in a game. Many games have high-score screens or other specialized information screens.

189

The very first things a player sees in a game are GUI elements. These elements might be simply loading screens, or they might be elaborate full-motion videos. The importance of making a favorable first impression on the player is obvious, so the need to design an interesting and visually impressive opening to a game goes without saying. The concept artist is responsible for creating a great opening for the game.

The most important aspect of an information screen is to give the player information. In the case of a legal screen, the information is spelled out in very specific legal text that needs to be clear. In the case of a title screen, the information might be more in the emotion of the art than in the text. Each screen in a game will have its own purpose. The concept artist needs to be aware of the purpose of each screen, and he must design the screen with that purpose in mind.

Some of the more common types of information screens are

- Title
- Loading
- Legal
- Level
- High-score
- Win
- Lose
- Credit

Title Screens

Title screens might be the most important of the information screens. At least content-wise, they are the screens that typically have the largest budgets. The title screen is the opening screen for a game; naturally, it includes the game's title. It is the screen that introduces the game to the player, and first impressions are very important.

A common practice in games is to have the title page use the same art as what is on the game box (if the game is sold at retail). Some online games don't have a box. If the game will be sold at retail, then the concept artist might wait to design the title page until the box art is designed. The main issue with using box art is that the box layout is different than a screen layout. Figure 11.1 shows the layout for retail boxes and game screens.

Notice that the box is either a vertical rectangle or a square. The screen, on the other hand, is a horizontal rectangle. Sometimes the box art will not look good when it is adapted for the title screen.

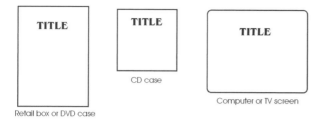

Figure 11.1
The layouts of boxes are different than that of the game screen.

In addition to the title screen, the game often will have an opening movie. Like the title screen, the movie is an information element in the game. If the game includes a movie, the concept artist will need to create a storyboard to explain the movie.

Loading Screens

Loading screens are also important initial screens in games. Games that are on either a CD or a DVD take time to load the game graphics into system memory. During the loading time, a loading screen is displayed on the screen. This screen can be as simple as a loading bar that grows as the game loads, or it can be much more. It is up to the designer and concept artist to decide what they want to put on the loading screen.

Some games get very creative with their loading screens. A racing game might have a car move across the screen instead of a loading bar. Some games even have simple little games that the player can play while he is waiting for the main game to load. Figure 11.2 shows a sketch for a racecar loading bar.

Figure 11.2
A racecar is used in the loading bar for this concept drawing.

Legal Screens

Legal screens have very specific legal requirements that make them a little less creative than other screens. A legal screen tells the player who owns what part of the game. The ownership is usually displayed as a trademark or copyright. There are specific requirements for displaying notices for both. Some games also might contain patented software, although that is less common.

Before designing a legal screen, it is a good idea to check with the attorney responsible for the game to get the legal text. The same attorney who makes sure the text is accurate should also check the concept design when it is completed.

In the case of a legal screen, the text should be clear and legible. The logos should be large enough to be recognizable. The composition should be simple and in most cases formal.

Level Screens

In many games, there is an introduction screen for each level. Often the level introduction screen is also a loading screen. Level screens are similar to title screens, with the exception that the level screen introduces the level and not the game. Level screens are often used in racing games, in which the level screen shows the layout of the upcoming course. Figure 11.3 shows a design for a level screen for a racing game.

Figure 11.3
Racing games often have level screens to introduce courses.

Unlike the title screen, one game might have a couple dozen level screens. The number of level screens is dependent on the number of levels in the game.

Some of the higher-budget games will have movies between levels. This doesn't happen too often because of the expense of creating FMV sequences, but the industry is moving more in that direction.

High-Score Screen

A high-score screen is a statistical screen that shows where the player's score is placed in relation to other players. High-score screens are similar to legal screens in that there is specific information that needs to be communicated. They are different from legal screens in that a lot more creativity can go into a high-score screen.

Win Screens

A win screen is the reward for the player when the game is won. Win screens need to be something special because the player has just spent a lot of time with the game. If the reward for winning is not very much, the player will be disappointed.

Lose Screens

A lose screen is like a win screen except that instead of winning the game, the player obviously has lost. Players often see lose screens several times during the course of playing the game, but the player only sees a win screen when he successfully completes the game. A lose screen obviously does not need to be a reward for the player, but it should encourage the player to return to the game and try again.

Credit Screens

As is the case with movies, a number of people contribute to the development of the game. Everyone who has a part in creating the game should be included in the credits for the game.

A credit screen lists the names and sometimes pictures of the people who contributed to the development of the game. Credits are very important to the development team, and there is a place in the credits for the concept artist. Credit screens have specific information, just like the legal and high-score screens. They are a little closer to the legal screens in that the credit information needs to be clear and easy to understand. However, they don't have the same specific wording requirements—although the members of the development team will be upset if their names or titles are incorrect!

Many people in the industry rely on credits to help them get work or upgrade their jobs. Some even become celebrities in gaming circles if they have worked on a popular title.

Menus

Menus are the most common GUI element for navigation. They are onscreen selection elements with selectable graphics that usually take the form of buttons (but can be other types of graphics as well). Each button on a menu has a function. The player navigates the game by selecting buttons with the game control device, which in the case of a PC game is usually the mouse. Figure 11.4 shows a design for a game options menu screen.

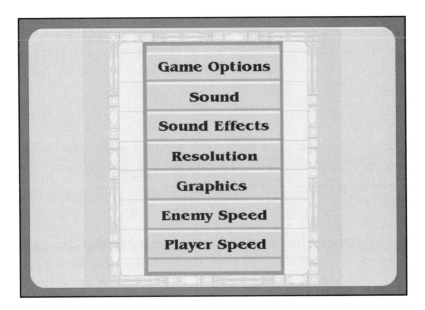

Figure 11.4
Most menu screens use buttons.

This example uses buttons to make selections. Buttons are virtual devices, and there is very little functional difference between a button and any other onscreen selectable item. The only real difference is in the animation of the button. There are several types of selectable elements that can be used in designing games. A few of them are

- Menu lists
- Buttons
- Icons
- Objects
- Characters

Menu Lists

The simplest form of menu is a list. Most people are familiar with menu lists in computer applications. The most common form of menu list is a pull-down menu; such menus usually are found at the top-left area of the screen. There are other types of menu lists as well, including marking menus and static lists. Marking menus float over the play screen and are accessed either by a mouse click or a button press on a game controller. Figure 11.5 shows a design using a marking menu on the left and a list menu on the right.

Figure 11.5
Marking menus are floating menus.

Menu lists are widely used in Internet and computer applications, but they are not as common in games, where a more graphically interesting approach is desirable.

Buttons

Buttons are graphic devices that have the appearance of a physical button. Many buttons are actually animated so that when the player activates one, it appears to be pressed. Figure 11.6 shows a button in its two stages of animation.

Buttons are common in games because they are visually more interesting than menu lists.

Figure 11.6
Many buttons are animated so their appearance changes when they are pressed.

Icons

Icons are very similar to buttons except that icons have small symbols or pictures. They can be pressed, similar to buttons, or they might simply change colors when selected. Figure 11.7 shows an example of an icon in the selected and non-selected states, with a simple color shift to indicate the difference.

Figure 11.7
Icons often use a color shift to indicate the selected or non-selected state.

Most people are familiar with icons from their use in computer software. The desktop of most operating systems contains multiple icons. Icons are used often in games because of their use of symbols. Often the symbol on an icon eliminates the need for text. The example in Figure 11.7 shows a child reading. The player doesn't need to have text that indicates the icon represents reading.

Objects

A very common practice in games is to use objects as interface devices. Unlike other interface devices, objects can exist as part of the game world. They don't have to be a separate interface device; they can be part of a setting. Doors leading from a room to play levels are an example of object interface art.

Many games have pickups—in-game elements that the player can acquire during game play. Pickups are not traditionally thought of as interface art because they are part of the actual game play. However, in many ways they act as interface devices because they are selectable items in a game.

As games become more advanced, the line between interface and game is becoming less defined. Game designers are starting to include many systems that were once interface elements in the game itself. This is really stretching the idea of a menu, but it is basically the same thing. For example, if a player selects the play level by selecting the door in a room, it is the same thing as selecting the level from a menu list. Menus do not have to be 2D word lists.

Characters

Using characters for selection items is similar in many ways to using objects, except that the character might be able to talk to the player to explain the selection. Selecting characters in a room is an obvious way to create a character selection menu. But characters can be used as selection items for more purposes than simply selecting characters. Characters are great for information. Using characters for interface elements is a lot more interesting than using a menu list.

Onscreen Displays

Many games have graphics that remain onscreen during game play. These graphics often give the player information about the game. They might indicate the health of a character or enemy, or they might show the speed of a vehicle. They might display the score or the number of items a player has collected. Their purpose is to give the player vital real-time information.

Onscreen displays are often called HUDs in the industry. *HUD* stands for *heads-up display*. The name comes from the displays used in military aircraft to give the pilot vital flight or enemy information while flying. Figure 11.8 is an example of a HUD for a racing game.

Figure 11.8
Racing games often have several HUD elements.

In Figure 11.8, there are three HUD elements. The upper-left corner contains the track display with the relative positions of each of the racers shown. The lower-left corner of the screen contains the position of the player. It indicates that the player is in first place. The lower-right part of the screen contains the speedometer. Each element has a purpose to help the player during the game.

It is very important to design the HUD carefully because the HUD is onscreen while the game is played. It is arguably the art that is seen most often by the player.

Concept artists need to be aware of the video safe area. The *video safe area* is the area not hidden by the game system. Some game systems do not display the full screen during the game. This is especially true for video game systems that display their signal on a standard TV. Computer games typically do not have this problem because they use a digital rather than an analog signal. As more display systems become digital, the need to worry about the video safe area will disappear. Figure 11.9 shows the video safe area of a TV video game.

When designing the HUD, the concept artist needs to place the onscreen elements in such a way that they do not interfere with the game action. The area where most of the game action takes place is called the *focal area*. Figure 11.10 shows the area used typically for the focal area of a game.

Figure 11.9
Some video game systems do not display the full game screen.

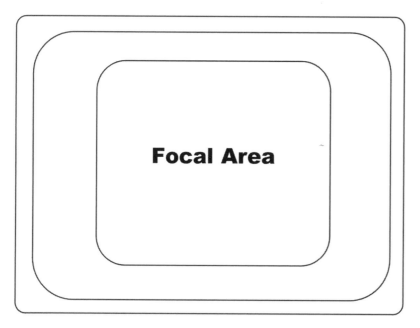

Figure 11.10
The center of the screen is usually the focal area.

The area between the focal area and the edge of the video safe area is the best location for placing HUD elements. Placing HUD elements in this area will make them less likely to intrude on the action of the game—but at the same time, they won't get cut off in some of the video game systems. Figure 11.11 shows the area where the HUD elements should go.

Figure 11.11
The area between the focal area and the video safe edge is the best location to place HUD elements.

Creating Game Navigation Design

This first example is a game options menu in a science-fiction adventure game. The design will use simple shapes. The first step is to define the screen area and lay in the background. In this case the background is a dark gradation, as shown in Figure 11.12.

hint

A vector-drawing program is a very useful tool for creating interface art designs. These art programs are very good at creating clean geometric shapes. They are also useful for laying down gradations or flat colors. More intricate drawings can be created in painting programs, and then imported into the vector program.

The next step is to create the basic menu areas. Draw in the shapes, as shown in Figure 11.13.

Figure 11.12
Start by defining the area of the screen.

Figure 11.13
Draw in the menu areas.

The central shape will be a monitor. Draw it in, as shown in Figure 11.14.

A character will speak to the player from the monitor. Add a character sketch to the monitor, as shown in Figure 11.15.

Figure 11.14
The center shape is a monitor.

Figure 11.15
Add a character sketch to the picture.

To give the design a more technical feel, add some tubes as support devices for the onscreen shapes. Figure 11.16 shows the tubes.

Now you can add the buttons to the picture, as shown in Figure 11.17.

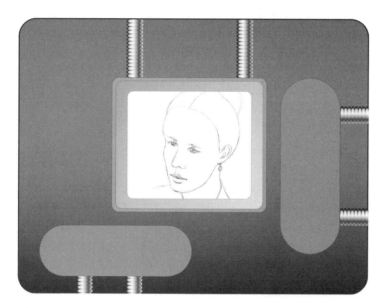

Figure 11.16
Add support devices to the drawing.

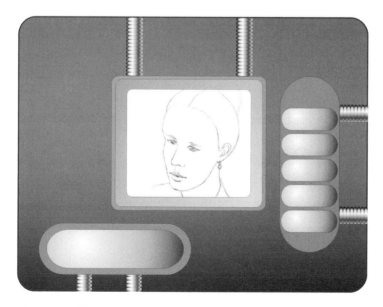

Figure 11.17
Add buttons to the shapes to create menu panels.

The last step to complete the concept sketch is to add the text to the buttons. Figure 11.18 shows the finished concept sketch of the game options screen.

Figure 11.18
Add the text to finish the game options sketch.

Creating Onscreen Elements

The next example is for a PC racing game HUD design. Because the game is for a PC, there is no need to deal with the video safe issue. The first step is to define the screen area, as shown in Figure 11.19.

HUDs are art that overlays the game. Add a sketch of a racing game to indicate what the game action will likely be, as shown in Figure 11.20.

Now you can add the HUD elements. The game design calls for an onscreen track layout that shows the progress of each car in the race. The first element you should add to the design is a miniature map of the track, as shown in Figure 11.21.

Now add small circles to the track to represent each car, as shown in Figure 11.22.

Figure 11.19
The first step is to define the dimensions of the screen.

Figure 11.20
Add a sketch of the game.

Figure 11.21
Next, add a miniature map of the track.

Figure 11.22
Add circles to the track to represent the cars.

The next HUD element is the position of the player. This element consists of bold text that indicates first, second, third, and fourth place in the race. Figure 11.23 shows this element added to the design.

The last element to add to the picture is the speedometer. This should be placed in the lower-right corner of the screen. The speedometer is a circular design, so the first step in building it is to create the shape, as shown in Figure 11.24.

Figure 11.23
Add the player's position in the race to the design.

Figure 11.24
Create the shape of the speedometer.

Add text indicating the levels of speed to the speedometer. The text should wrap around the inside of the circle, similar to a real speedometer, as shown in Figure 11.25.

The last element to add is an indicator of how fast the racecar is traveling. You can do this by adding a needle to the speedometer, as shown in Figure 11.26.

Figure 11.25
Add the speeds to the speedometer.

Figure 11.26
Add a needle to show how fast the car is going.

Summary

This chapter has given you a very basic overview of interface art design and creation. However, the subject deserves much more attention than this book can give it. This chapter covered several concepts regarding interface art. In addition, it showed examples of creating concept art for interfaces. It also categorized interface art into information, navigation, and onscreen art, and provided explanations for each.

In this chapter, you should have learned the following concepts:

- What the different types of interface art are, including title, loading, legal, level, high-score, win, lose, and credit screens
- What different types of selection elements you can use, including menu lists, buttons, icons, objects, and characters
- How to create a design for a menu screen
- How to create a design for a heads-up display

Questions

1. What does GUI stand for?
2. How does the player receive game information?
3. What are information screens?
4. What is a title screen?
5. What is a loading screen?
6. What is the loading bar used for?
7. Why is there less creativity in creating legal screens than other information screens?
8. How are level screens and title screens similar?
9. What are high-score screens?
10. Who is listed in the credits of a game?
11. What are menus?
12. What is a marking menu?
13. Why are word list menus seldom used in games?
14. What advantage does an icon have over a button?
15. Can interface elements be incorporated into the natural play of the game?

Answers

1. Graphical user interface.

2. Through interface elements in a game.

3. Screens that give the player specific game information.

4. The opening screen for a game, which includes the title of the game.

5. The screen that appears when the game is loading.

6. To indicate the progress of the loading of the game.

7. Legal screens have specific legal requirements.

8. They are both introduction screens.

9. Statistical screens that show the player's score versus other players' scores.

10. Everyone who has a part in creating the game should be included in the credits for the game.

11. Onscreen selection elements with selectable graphics. The graphics are usually in the form of buttons, but there can be other types of graphics as well.

12. A floating menu.

13. Word lists are not as interesting as other forms of graphics.

14. Because icons use symbols, they might not need text to explain their purpose.

15. Yes.

Discussion Questions

1. Why is the title screen one of the most important screens in the game?

2. Why should the concept artist check with legal counsel when creating the legal screen?

3. Why would a concept artist not use menu word lists?

4. What should a concept artist consider when creating the HUD for a game?

5. What are some creative ways to hide menus within the game?

Exercises

1. Create a title screen for a sports game. Make the title dynamic so it gives the viewer a sense of action.

2. Create a unique loading screen for an adventure game. Do something creative with the loading bar to make it more interesting.

3. Create a HUD for a military tank game. Give the HUD a very military look. Make sure it is safe for video and does not encroach on the focal area.

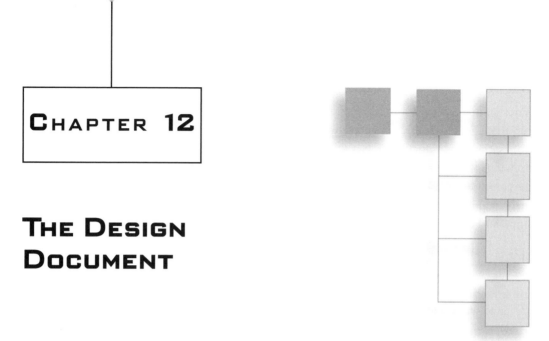

CHAPTER 12

THE DESIGN DOCUMENT

As important as the concept art is, it doesn't do much good if the design document is not well designed. The design document is the vehicle that houses all of the concept art. A well-designed design document is expected in the industry. This chapter will help you create design documents. It will include topics such as understanding design documents; developing themes, covers, and title pages; working with fonts; and designing page layouts.

The design document is just as much a work of art as any picture created for the game design. In fact, in some ways it is the most important work of art because it gives the first impression of the game. A potential publisher or investor is introduced to the game through the design document.

Creating a design document is different than designing a game. There is a whole discipline of art called graphic design that is devoted to designing documents. This chapter does not contain all of the concepts involved with designing documents; such an explanation is beyond the scope of this book. Instead, this chapter should be thought of as a foundation for the artist.

Understanding Design Documents

A design document is a lot of things. First and most important, a design document is an organized repository of conceptual ideas for the game. Second, a design document is a road map for the development of the game. Third, a design document is a promotional tool for the game.

The Design Document as a Repository

A design document is sometimes referred to as the game bible. This reference is due to the fact that the design document contains all of the conceptual ideas for the game. In other words, the design document is a reference manual for the game. All of the finished charts, drawings, storyboards, illustrations, and sketches discussed in this book are included in the game design document. In addition, the design document contains extensive text about the game, including production charts, task lists, asset lists, game play descriptions, back story, and cost estimates.

hint

Other than the formatting of the text portions of the document, this book will not deal with the written content of the game design document. For more information on the written portions of the design document, you should refer to books specifically about game design. However, you should be familiar with the written portion from the standpoint of knowing where and how each section fits into the design document. If you want to know more about game design, I suggest you pick up Bob Bates' book *Game Design: The Art and Business of Creating Games* (Premier Press, 2002).

The size and scope of every game design document is different. The designer is usually in charge of specifying the contents of the document based on the game and the needs of the project. It is the concept artist's job to design the look of the document.

The Design Document as a Roadmap

A roadmap helps you understand how to get from one location to another. In the case of a game design document, the idea is to help the development team get from the concept of the game to a finished product. The design document goes beyond simply telling the design team the way to go from one point to another; it also gives the team all of the important information for the trip.

A good design document anticipates all of the major and many of the minor tasks that need to be completed to create the game. It gives examples to guide the art production staff in creating game assets. It also gives examples (or at least specifies the needs) for every aspect of the game.

Game design documents must be detailed to be effective. The detail can create extensive documents, sometimes numbering in the hundreds or thousands of pages!

The Design Document as a Promotion Tool

A game design document is often used to promote a game. The promotion is not usually to the general game buyers; rather, it is to those persons who control whether the game will be published. This includes a number of people, such as investors, publishers, corporate executives, and others involved in the publishing decisions. Sometimes these people review a number of game designs to find a few into which they want to put the time and effort of development. Catching their attention with a well-designed document could mean the difference between starting game production and shelving the game idea.

If it were not for the promotional aspects of creating a game design document, the need for creative design of documents would not be as important. The promotional aspects of game design documents are what really drive the entire document design agenda. The development team simply needs a working document.

Developing Themes

The first step in designing a game design document is coming up with a visual theme or motif for the document. A visual theme or motif is an overriding design that ties the document together. It includes the style of the type, organization of the items on individual pages, and any design elements that flow throughout the documents.

Themes should reflect the content of the design document. A medieval fantasy game should have a theme that reflects a medieval time period. A futuristic science fiction game should have a theme that gives the impression of a futuristic time period. A western game should not have a 1950s detective thriller theme.

Sometimes the concept art will suggest a theme for the design document, but more often than not, it is a good idea to have the theme in mind before the concept art is created. The design document contains most (if not all) of the finished concept art. The concept art should match or at least fit well with the theme of the document. This means that if the game is a horror fantasy game, a slick marker rendering of the art might not be appropriate. The best documents have a consistent feel between the document theme and the individual pieces of art.

There are many ways to develop a theme for a document. One way is to create an environment for the document to reside, kind of like a house that contains the graphics and text of the document. Figure 12.1 shows this approach. Each page is printed with a star-field motif. The game obviously takes place in outer space.

Figure 12.1
This motif is for a game that takes place in outer space.

The nice part about this example is that there is no question about the theme of the game. The reader can tell that it is a space game just by looking at the document, even without reading a word.

A document theme is more than just a background picture. It conveys the overall look and feel of the document. The fonts, the layout, and the subject headings (in short, everything in the document) affect how it is perceived and, therefore, they are part of the theme. Figure 12.2 shows the addition of the headings and subheadings to the document.

When developing themes for a design document, the concept artist should start with the game. One good way to look at the creation of a theme for the game document is to think of the game and imagine, "If this game were a document, what would it look like?" The theme of the document should reflect what the game is and, in many ways, it should look like the game. If there is an overall artistic theme for the game, which there should be, then that theme should carry through to the document.

Figure 12.2
The theme is continued through the headings and subheadings.

Designing Covers

The document cover is the very first thing seen by anyone who wants to read it. It provides the reader with his first impression of the document, and it should really catch the reader's attention. The cover is the outside first page of a document. It is usually part of the binding if the document is in physical form, or it is the first page of an electronic document. It may or may not list the title of the game.

hint

Increasingly, game documents are becoming electronic documents rather than paper ones. The advantages of electronic documents are that they can be sent over the Internet, and they can contain elements that paper cannot, such as sound. An electronic document is also perceived as more progressive.

This is not to say that every design document should be electronic. A physical document can sometimes be very impressive simply because of the tactile nature of its presence.

Because the cover gives the first impression of a document, it needs to be an attention-getting work of art. In Figure 12.3, the game is an off-road racing game. The focus on the close-up of tire impressions and the play on the words "dirt" and "track" make for an attention-getting cover. The reader is in fact looking at tracks in the dirt.

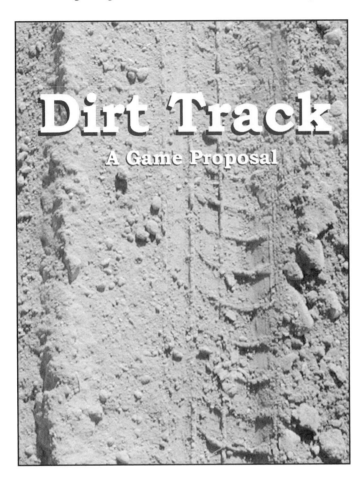

Figure 12.3
The close-up of the dirt makes this an attention-getting cover.

There is nothing that says a game design document has to be an 8 1/2 × 11-inch portrait-oriented document. Although that is the most common format for a document, a game design document can be any size or shape that works. The cover of the document does not have to contain a title. Figure 12.4 shows a design document in a landscape format. The document uses a close-up of an elephant's eye as its cover.

This document stands out in a crowd of same-size, same-format documents. It shows creativity and ingenuity. In short, it is the type of document cover that grabs interest.

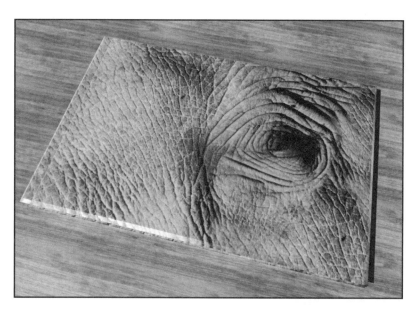

Figure 12.4
This document has an elephant's eye on its cover.

Designing Title Pages

Titles and covers for documents are closely related. In some documents they are the same thing; the title page acts as the cover. Many of the issues regarding a cover's design apply to the title page, with the exception that the title page always has the title of the game and should include the author of the document or the company that created it.

Title pages are a little like the overture of a symphony; they give a visual introduction to the game design document. Whether the message is subtle or blatant, the title page should give the reader of the document an indication of what is to come. Figure 12.5 shows a title page created by artist Tim Huntzenger for a game design document.

When you are designing a title page, there is a hierarchy of importance to the elements on the page. The highest priority and first focal point of the page should be the game title. In this example, the title is written in large type across the top of the page. It is in an area that is uncluttered by other elements. After the title, the next area of focus is the picture, which is dynamic and full of action. The lower part of the illustration has the car bursting from the picture, and it attracts the viewer's attention. The third area of attention is the author's name, which is written across the bottom of the page—in this case, it is Alpine Studios. Figure 12.6 shows the three areas of interest.

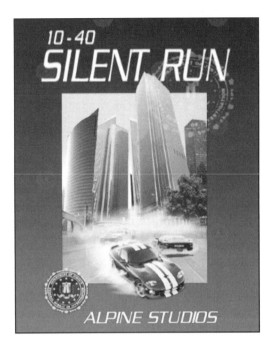

Figure 12.5
Title pages should highlight the game's title.

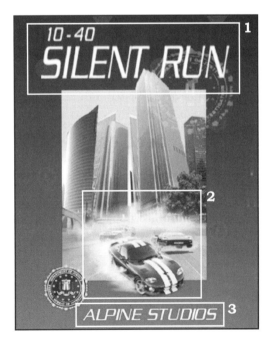

Figure 12.6
This title page has three areas of focus.

Working with Fonts

One of the most important considerations for the design document is the font, which can have a dramatic impact on the look of a document. Just by changing the font, you can change a document from formal to casual or from modern to archaic. In Figure 12.7, the same paragraph is written in several different fonts. Notice how the same words can have a different feel when you change the font.

The type font can have a dramatic effect on the look of a document. The feel of a document can change completely just by the use of type.

The type font can have a dramatic effect on the look of a document. The feel of a document can change completely just by the use of type.

The type font can have a dramatic effect on the look of a document. The feel of a document can change completely just by the use of type.

The type font can have a dramatic effect on the look of a document. The feel of a document can change completely just by the use of type.

The type font can have a dramatic effect on the look of a document. The feel of a document can change completely just by the use of type.

Figure 12.7
You can make the same words look very different just by changing the font.

When choosing a font for your document, you should consider both readability and style of the font.

Readability

Some fonts that work well for headings do not work very well for body type. In Figure 12.7, the font in the center is the most readable in body copy, while the two fonts at the bottom of the page are the least readable for body copy. The issue with body copy is that often the font is a 10- or 12-point size. When placed in a large block of type, some fonts will read well while others will be difficult to read.

There are two basic fonts—serif and sans serif. A serif is the small flare that some fonts have on the ends of each letter or number, while a sans serif font has no flares at the ends of letters and numbers. Figure 12.8 shows two fonts. The top one is a sans serif font, and the bottom one is a serif font.

Figure 12.8
Some fonts have serifs, and others do not.

Most of us grew up reading schoolbooks printed with serif fonts. Schoolbooks use serif fonts because they tend to be easier to read in block copy. The small serifs make each letter or number easier to define. This is not to say that sans serif fonts are not easy to read in general; it is only to say that serif fonts usually are easier to read than sans serif fonts in blocks of type.

When you create a heading, the opposite might be true. Serifs are helpful in body copy because the serif better defines the letter or number. However, when the typeface is large, the need for the serif is not as critical. The boldness of a clean shape in large type often creates a stronger image than a serif typeface.

Style

In the olden days, printing was done with a piece of metal with a letter or number cast on one end. Each letter had to be placed individually. The number of styles available to the designer back then was very limited. In fact, some printers only had one style, and thus everything was printed in that style.

Today, computer technology has allowed for almost an unlimited number of fonts. The biggest problem an artist runs into when selecting a font is choosing from all the possibilities. Figure 12.9 shows a range of styles. It is just a small cross-section of thousands of fonts available.

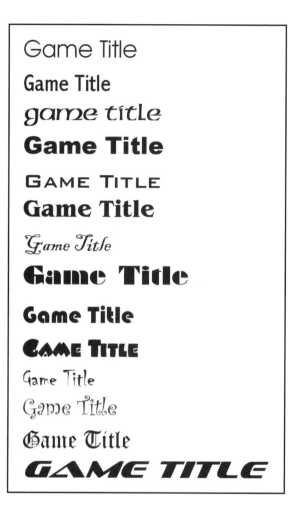

Figure 12.9
This shows only a few of the many fonts from which the concept artist can choose.

Notice the variety of fonts in only the few samples shown in Figure 12.9. Each font in this example could be used for a game title. Some are more appropriate for some games than others. For example, the bottom four typefaces have very different feels to them. The bottom one could work well in a racing game. The next one up would not work well for a racing game, unless the game was medieval cart racing, because the font is a very old-style font. The next one up is a whimsical font that could be used in a lighthearted party game. It is very different from the one above it, which looks like a good candidate for a horror game.

The concept artist should pick the fonts that best communicate the nature of the game while still being readable.

Page Layout

Page layout is the process of creating the look of each individual page. Laying out each page is a matter of arranging the text and graphics into a consistent whole. Each page should follow the theme of the game mentioned earlier. The layout should include text that is easy to read and graphics that enhance the document.

One of the biggest jobs in page layout is placing the graphics. Each graphic should be placed near the text that explains it. The reader should be able to read the document and look at the graphics in an orderly manner, without any question as to why a particular graphic is in a specific place.

Layout Styles

Making dummy pages is a good way to test out the look of the layout before a specific layout style is instituted. The following examples will explore several layout styles. The layouts in the examples are dummy layouts. A *dummy layout* allows the artist to quickly experiment with styles to see how they will look. The advantage to using dummy layouts instead of formatting the text and pictures is the same as the advantage to creating thumbnail sketches before you create a picture: You can work out the design without a major time commitment.

Formal

In the formal style, the document is perfectly balanced. Like the formal compositions discussed earlier in the book, the formal style is one in which all of the graphics are centered on the page. Figure 12.10 shows an example of a formal layout.

The formal style works great for some documents, but it is very proper, which does not always work for a game design. It might work for a game design dealing with traditional chess, but most games will need a more dynamic page layout.

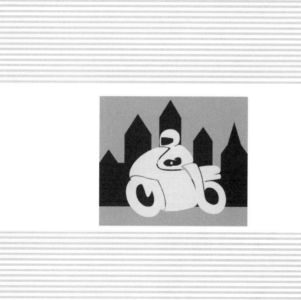

Figure 12.10
The formal style has perfect balance.

Diagonal

In the diagonal style, the graphics are offset from each other in a diagonal manner. This offset can go either from right to left or from left to right. Figure 12.11 shows a diagonal layout going from left to right.

The diagonal style is more dynamic than the formal style, but it has its drawbacks. The diagonal style calls for two graphics per page, which can cause problems when graphics and text don't match up.

Figure 12.11
The diagonal style has graphics on opposite sides of the page.

Staggered

The staggered style is similar to the diagonal style except that the graphics are placed next to the text that deals with them. The graphics are staggered from one side of the page to the other. Figure 12.12 shows a staggered style.

The staggered layout is one of the most commons styles, but it does have a few problems. One is that there might be several pictures on one page and none on another. This creates a kind of tattered layout with little consistency between pages.

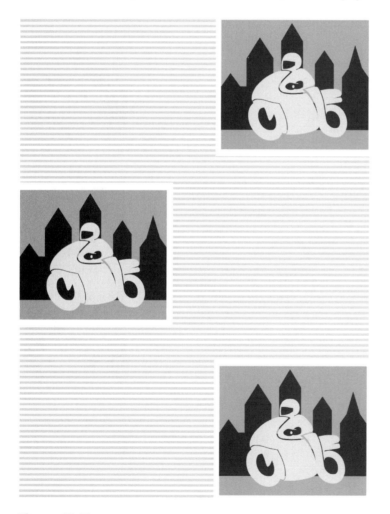

Figure 12.12
The staggered style places pictures next to the text that describes them.

Flush

A flush style places all the graphics on one side of the page or another. The flush style is more static, similar to the formal style, but not as balanced because the pictures line up on one side. Figure 12.13 shows the flush style with the graphics on the left side of the page.

The problem with the flush-left approach is that the pictures tend to fight with the headings. Figure 12.14 shows a flush-right style.

The flush approach to page layout can be problematic because it is unbalanced and the text sometimes gets lost between the graphics.

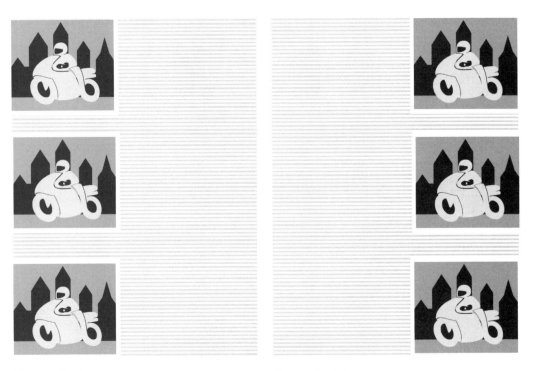

Figure 12.13
The flush style lines up the pictures on one side of the page.

Figure 12.14
The flush-right style places the pictures on the right side of the page.

Two-Column Flush

Creating two columns on a page helps to resolve some of the text problems with a flush design. It also makes the text easier to follow because the lines of text are not so long horizontally. The reader will not have as much of a problem picking up the text from one line to the next. Figure 12.15 shows a flush-right design with a two-column approach. The left column is devoted to text, and the right column is devoted to graphics.

The graphics in this design can be placed next to the description text, or they can be placed in a specific location on the page, such as at the top. This design is nice and airy, but it still has balance problems, and it can use a lot more paper than other designs.

Figure 12.15
The two-column flush design solves some of the text problems of a flush style.

Two-Column Random

The two-column random style is just what the name implies—the graphics are placed in the column whenever they are called for in the text. Figure 12.16 shows this type of design.

Two-column random is a common design motif because the smaller column width is easier to read, and the pictures correspond to the text. The problems with this style are the same as those associated with the staggered style—there might be several pictures on one page and none on others.

Figure 12.16
Two-column random places the pictures wherever they come up in the text.

Other Styles

The number of page layout styles is limited only by the artist's imagination. I have presented only a few, but they represent some of the more common approaches to page layout.

Special Page-Layout Considerations

Some pages in the game design document will not work well for a consistent layout design. Pages that contain large, complex tables or charts will present a layout challenge to the concept artist, as will pages with extensive asset lists. The best way to deal with these special-case pages is to reserve sections of the document for them in which they can be designed in groups. For instance, the asset lists can have a section, and the charts can have a section. Then, each section of the document can have its own consistent design.

Summary

This chapter has been a crash course in graphic design as it relates to game design documents. It is by no means a thorough exploration of the topic. Graphic design is an art discipline with its own world of issues. An artist can spend his entire life studying graphic design and still not cover everything. My hope is that this chapter will help you get started designing compelling design documents.

In this chapter, you should have learned the following concepts:

- What design documents are
- The importance of themes in your design documents
- How to create covers for your design documents
- How to create title pages for your design documents
- The importance of choosing fonts
- How to choose a page layout for your design document
- The difference between some possible page layout styles, including formal, diagonal, staggered, flush, two-column flush, and two-column random layouts

Questions

1. What school of art deals with document layout?
2. What is the first and most important aspect of a game design document?
3. What is the second most important aspect of a game design document?
4. What is the third most important aspect of a game design document?
5. What art is included in the game design document?

6. True or false: A good design document will anticipate all of the major and many of the minor tasks that need to be completed to create the game.

7. What really drives the design of the game design document?

8. What do you call an overriding design that ties together the document?

9. What in the game design document affects its theme?

10. Why is the cover of a document so important?

11. Does a cover always need to contain a title?

12. What should be the focal point of a title page?

13. True or false: The readability of a font is the same whether it is used in a large heading or a block of copy.

14. Creating the look of each individual page is called what?

15. Why do two-column designs improve the readability of a document?

Answers

1. Graphic design.

2. It is an organized repository of conceptual ideas for the game.

3. It is a road map for the development of the game.

4. It is a promotional tool for the game.

5. All of the finished charts, drawings, storyboards, illustrations, and sketches relating to the game.

6. True.

7. The promotional aspects of the document's purpose.

8. The theme or motif of the document.

9. Everything.

10. It provides the reader with his first impression of the document.

11. No.

12. The title.

13. False.

14. Page layout.

15. The reader is less likely to get lost going from one line to the next.

Discussion Questions

1. Why is the look of the game design document important?
2. What is a game design document used for?
3. How does the game design document help the development team?
4. What are the advantages and disadvantages of electronic documents?
5. What is the best page layout for game design? Why?

Exercises

1. Create a game design document for your favorite game. Use graphics from the game for the pictures in the document
2. Create a cover for a game design document. The reader should be able to tell the type of game by simply looking at the cover.
3. Create dummy page layouts for a racing game, a fighting game, and a puzzle game. Explain why the layout works best for each game.

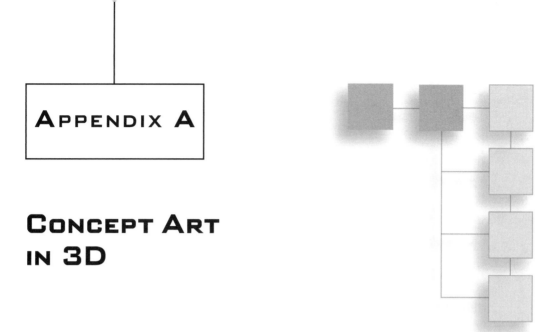

Appendix A

Concept Art in 3D

Some artists have taken the step to create concept art in 3D for 3D games. This approach generally takes longer but is better from the standpoint that it more closely approximates the final product. Three-dimensional concept art also has an advantage because small adjustments to 3D art are relatively easy to make. This allows the concept artist to explore colors and other changes without having to completely redraw the art.

For the following example, I've used a 3D program called Maya to create the 3D concept art. You can download a free learning edition of Maya from http://www.alias.com. Go to the download area and look for the PLE version of Maya.

There are several texture files used in this project, all of which are available for download at http://www.courseptr.com/downloads.

Building a Game Board

I chose a simple object so you would be able to follow the process of creating 3D concept art even if you're a beginner. Bring up Maya to begin the project.

1. The first step is to create a polygon plane. A *plane* is one of several polygon primitives supported by Maya. To set the options for the plane, bring up the Polygon Plane Options dialog box by selecting Polygon Primitives, Plane from the Create menu, as shown in Figure A.1.

2. Set the options in the dialog box to match those shown in Figure A.2, and click on the Apply button. A new polygon plane will appear.

3. The work area in Maya is called the *panel*, and it has its own menu. Go to the Panel menu in the upper-left corner of the work area and change the view to the Top view by selecting Panel, Orthographic, Top.

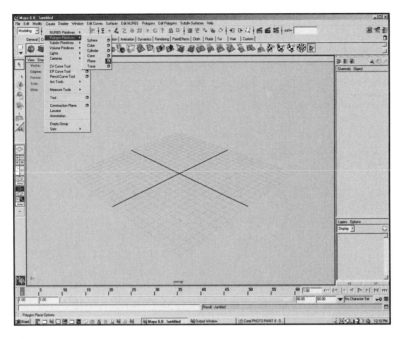

Figure A.1
Select Polygon Primitives, Plane to bring up the Polygon Plane Options dialog box.

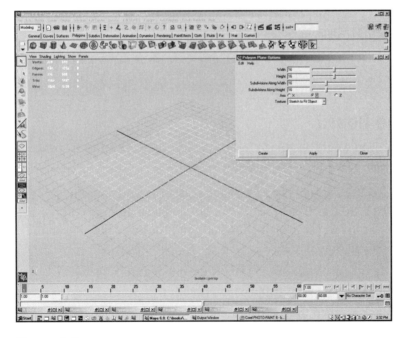

Figure A.2
A new polygon plane will appear after you click on Apply.

4. With the new plane selected, right-click and hold on one of the lines in the new plane object. A marking menu will appear. Choose Edge and release the mouse button. Now Edges will be the active selection mode.

5. Select all the edges around the outside of the plane, as shown in Figure A.3. The selected edges will be orange.

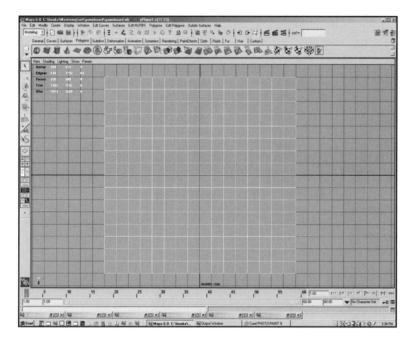

Figure A.3
Select the edges around the outside of the plane.

6. Return to the Perspective view by selecting Panel, Perspective, Perspective.

7. The next step is to extrude the sides of the plane upward. Before you do so, set the faces so they remain together by selecting Polygons, Tool Options, Keep Faces Together.

8. Now select Extrude Edge from the Edit Polygons menu, as shown in Figure A.4.

9. Move the extruded edges upward, as shown in Figure A.5. The Move tool is on the left side of the screen, and it is designated by an icon that shows an arrow next to a cone. In Figure A.5, it is highlighted by a box around the button. Click on the green arrow and drag the edges upward.

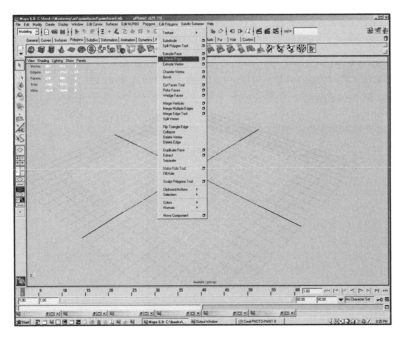

Figure A.4
The Extrude Edge option is in the Edit Polygons menu.

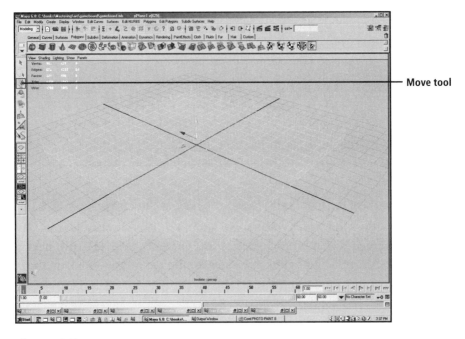

Move tool

Figure A.5
Move the edges upward.

10. Now extrude the edges again and move them upward just a little more.

11. Use the Scale tool to scale the extruded edges outward, as shown in Figure A.6. The Scale tool is also on the left side of the screen; it is designated by a button that shows a cube and two red arrows, and it is highlighted in Figure A.6 by a box around the button. Click on the center box and drag the mouse to the right.

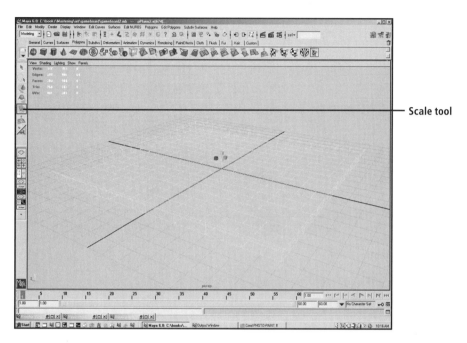

— Scale tool

Figure A.6
Scale the extruded edges outward.

12. Extrude the edges again and scale them outward without moving them upward, as shown in Figure A.7. Scale them a little more than the last step.

13. Extrude the edges again.

14. Now move the edges down until they are even with the top of the first extrusion.

15. Scale the edges outward, as shown in Figure A.8. Try to make them symmetrical with the polygons on the other side.

16. Extrude the edges again and pull them downward so they end up just below the original plane, as shown in Figure A.9.

The model for the game board is finished. Now it is time to give the model some textures.

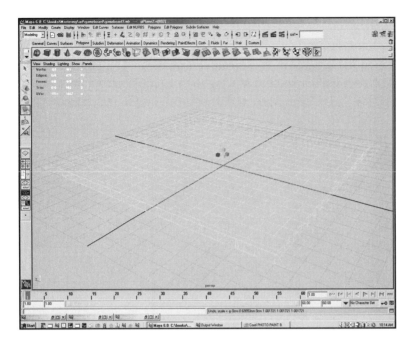

Figure A.7
Scale the extruded edges again.

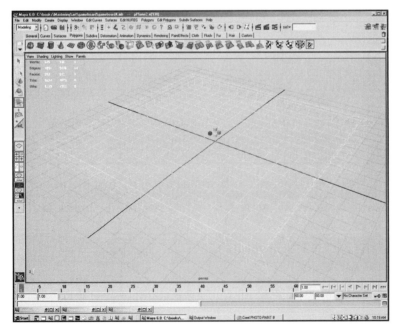

Figure A.8
Try to make the edges symmetrical.

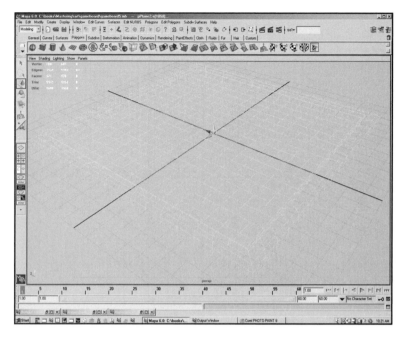

Figure A.9
Extrude the edges and pull them downward.

Texturing the Game Board

Maya has an advanced system of materials for texturing models. Materials in Maya describe much more than simply a picture pasted on a polygon. Materials can have many other attributes, including transparency, reflectivity, specularity, bump, luminance, and more.

1. Maya uses an editor called Hypershade to create and edit materials. Bring up Hypershade by selecting Window, Rendering Editors, Hypershade, as shown in Figure A.10.

2. Create a new material by selecting Create, Materials, Blinn in the Hypershade menu, as shown in Figure A.11.

3. With the new material selected, select Attribute Editor from the Window menu, as shown in Figure A.12.

4. The Attribute Editor will appear on the right side of the screen, as shown in Figure A.13. Under Common Material Attributes, there are several options for cus-tomizing the material. The first option is for material color. To the far right of the Color slider, you'll see a checkered icon button. Click on this button.

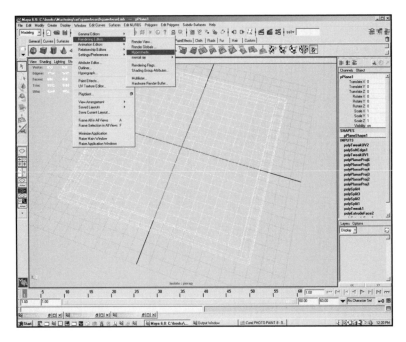

Figure A.10
Hypershade is a rendering editor.

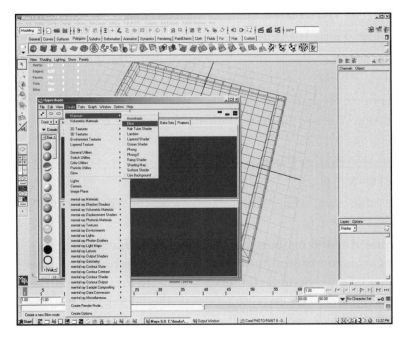

Figure A.11
Create a new material.

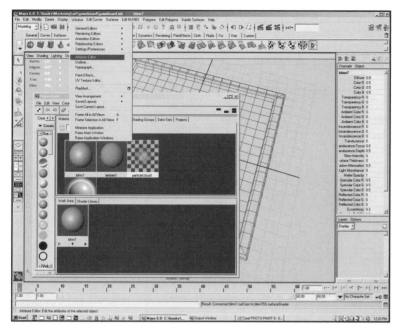

Figure A.12
The Attribute Editor is located in the Window menu.

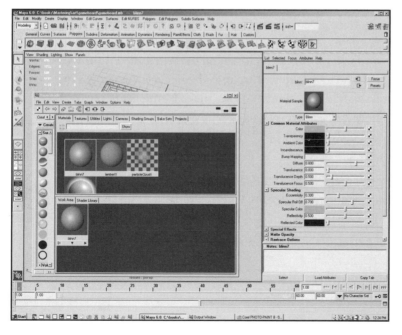

Figure A.13
The Attribute Editor has several options for customizing the material.

5. A Create Render Node dialog box will appear, as shown in Figure A.14. Click on the button labeled File.

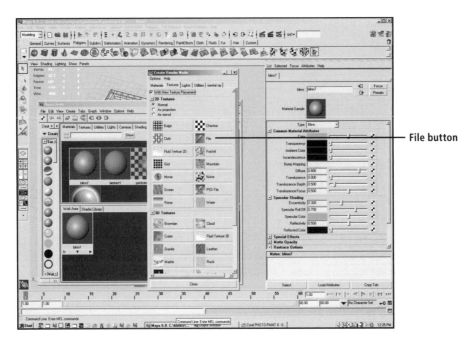

Figure A.14
Click on File in the Create Render Node dialog box.

6. The Create Render Node dialog box will close, and the Attribute Editor will change to allow you to load a bitmap texture into the material, as shown in Figure A.15. Click on the folder icon next to the Image Name field.

7. A load image dialog box will appear. Browse to the texture files you downloaded from http://www.courseptr.com/downloads and select WOODgold.bmp. Click on the Load button.

8. Change the name of the material by right-clicking on the material in Hypershade. This will bring up a marking menu. Choose Rename from the marking menu.

9. Change the material name to woodgold, as shown in Figure A.16.

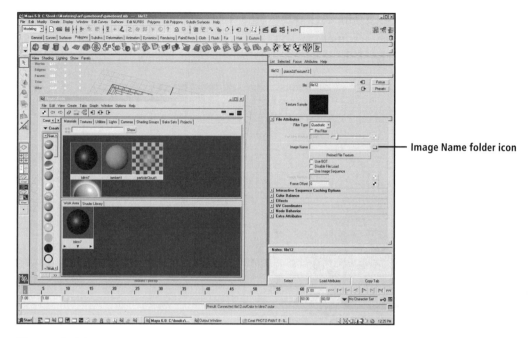

Image Name folder icon

Figure A.15
Click on the Image Name folder icon.

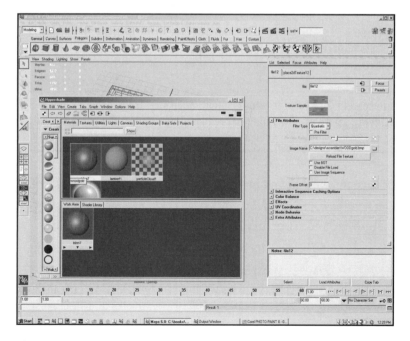

Figure A.16
Change the name of the material to woodgold.

10. Repeat Steps 1 through 9 for each of the other texture files you downloaded for this project. Rename each new material so that it is the same as the texture file name. Figure A.17 shows Hypershade with all of the new materials for the project loaded.

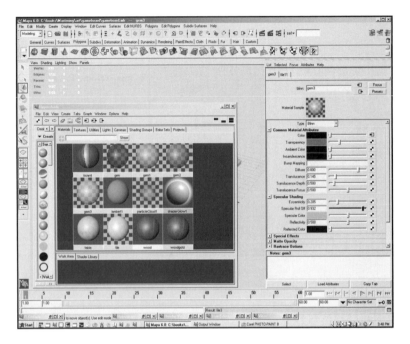

Figure A.17
Load all of the texture files for the project.

hint

The gem materials are transparent. To make them transparent, adjust the Transparency slider in the Attribute Editor about halfway before you load the texture files. This will give the gem materials a transparent look.

11. Press the 6 key to change the view to Smooth Shaded. The model should now look like Figure A.18.

12. Change the view to Top view and select all of the faces of the original flat plane.

13. Bring up Hypershade and right-click on the board material to bring up the marking menu. Select Apply Material to Selected to apply the material to the selected faces.

14. Bring up the Polygon Planar Projection Options dialog box by selecting Edit Polygons, Texture, Planar Mapping, as shown in Figure A.19.

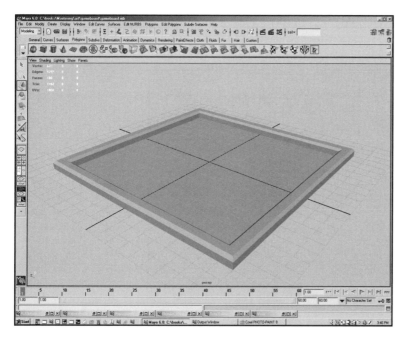

Figure A.18
Change the view to Smooth Shaded.

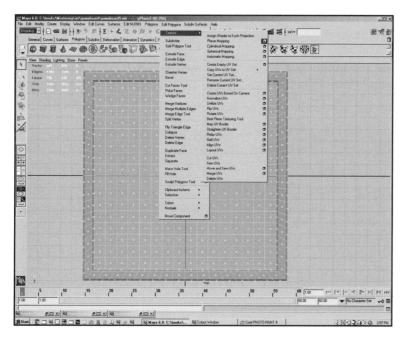

Figure A.19
Bring up the Polygon Planar Projection Options dialog box.

15. Set the options in the dialog box to those shown in Figure A.20, and click on Apply. The model should now look like Figure A.20.

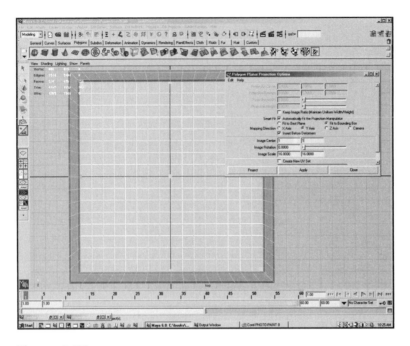

Figure A.20
Apply the board material to the model.

16. Select the faces of the top of the board border, as shown in Figure A.21. Make sure the top faces are selected (not the sides). You will apply a material to the sides later.

17. Apply the woodgold material to the selected faces.

18. Change the settings in the Polygon Planar Projection Options dialog box to those shown in Figure A.22, and click on Apply to arrange the textures for the board border.

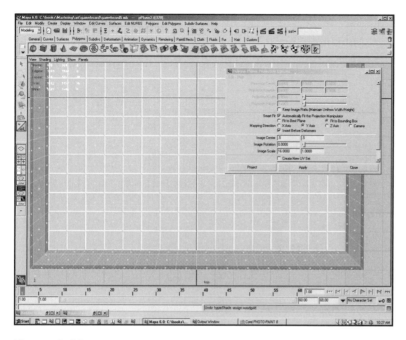

Figure A.21
Select the top faces of the board border.

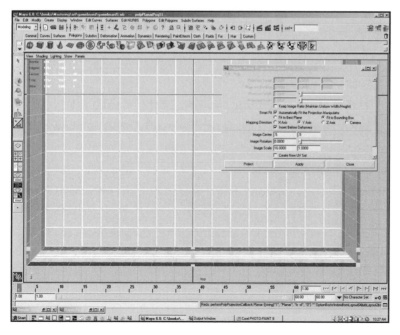

Figure A.22
Change the settings in the Polygon Planar Projection Options dialog box.

19. Now select the top faces along the side of the model and apply the woodgold material, the same way you did in Step 17.

20. Set the options in the Polygon Planar Projection Options dialog box to those shown in Figure A.23.

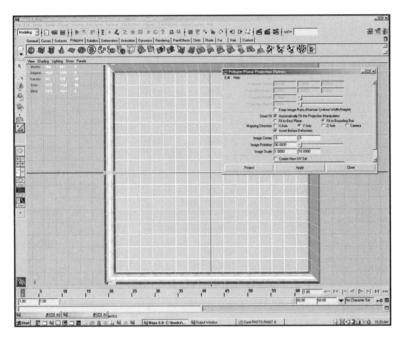

Figure A.23
Change the settings in the Polygon Planar Projection Options dialog box for the side of the board border.

21. Apply the woodgold texture to the remaining two sides of the board border.

22. From the Front view, select the faces of the sides of the board border, as shown in Figure A.24.

23. Apply the wood material to the selected faces.

24. Use the Polygon Planar Projection Options dialog box and set the options as shown in Figure A.25.

25. Now go to the Side view and project the wood texture onto the side faces of the board border in the same way you did in Steps 22 through 24, but change the projection axis to X instead of Z.

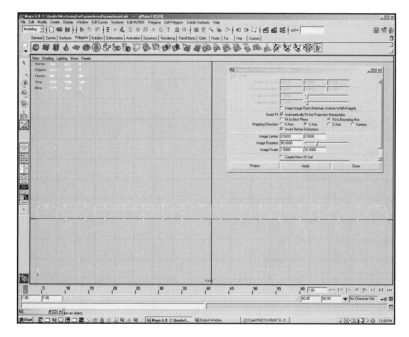

Figure A.24
Select the faces of the sides of the board border.

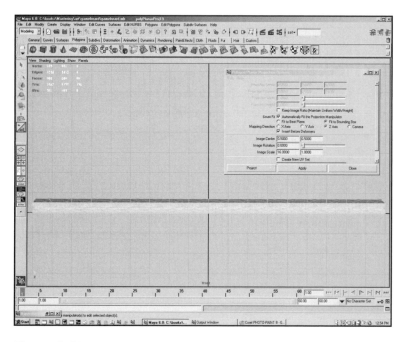

Figure A.25
Project the wood texture onto the sides of the board border.

The model of the game board is now textured. It should look similar to Figure A.26. In the next part of the project, you will add the game pieces to the model.

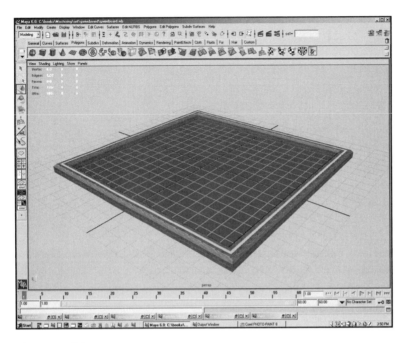

Figure A.26
The textured game board

Adding the Game Pieces

The game pieces will be modified polygon sphere primitives. The spheres are created in the same way as the polygon plane was in the beginning of this project.

1. Bring up the Polygon Sphere Options dialog box.

2. Set the options to those shown in Figure A.27.

3. Move the sphere to the corner of the game board, as shown in Figure A.28. Make sure the game piece is centered on the one of the squares of the board. Use the Scale tool to flatten the game piece, as shown in Figure A.28.

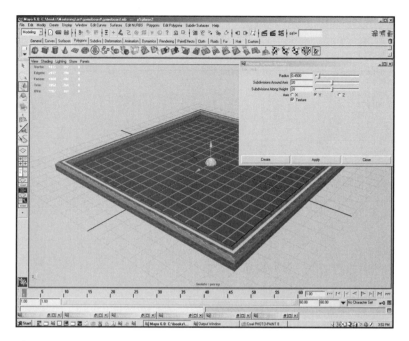

Figure A.27
Create a polygon sphere.

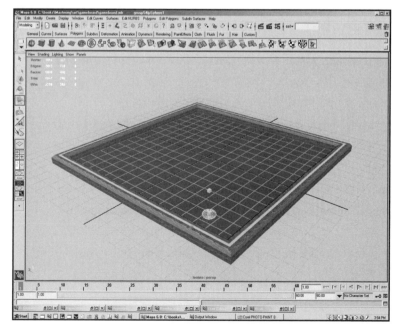

Figure A.28
Scale the game piece so it is flattened instead of round.

4. Use the Planar Mapping tool to project the gem material on the game piece, as shown in Figure A.29.

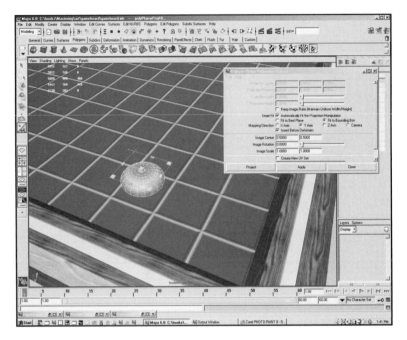

Figure A.29
Project the gem texture onto the game piece.

5. Duplicate the game piece by pressing Ctrl+D. Move the duplicated game piece on the square to the side.

6. Repeat Step 5 two more times, until there are four game pieces.

7. Select one of the game pieces and bring up Hypershade. Select the gem1 material and apply it to the selected game piece.

8. Apply the gem2 material to another piece.

9. Apply the gem3 material to a different piece.

10. Move the game pieces to the different sides of the game board, as shown in Figure A.30.

11. Duplicate the game pieces and fill in the squares, as shown in Figure A.31.

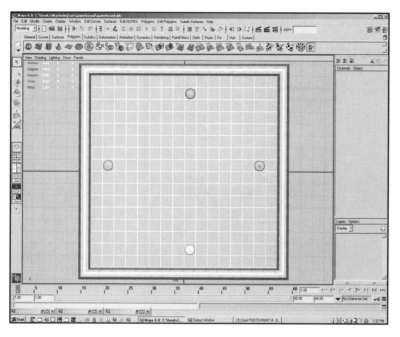

Figure A.30
Move the game pieces to the sides of the game board.

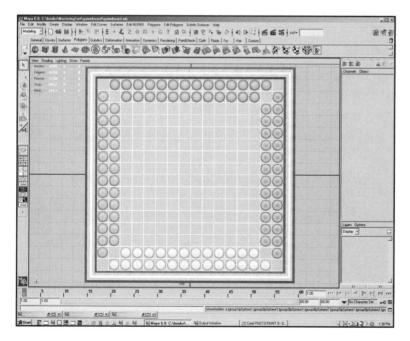

Figure A.31
Fill in the game board with game pieces.

The game board is now finished with game pieces; it should look similar to Figure A.32.

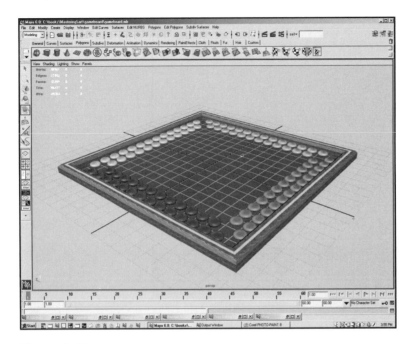

Figure A.32
The finished game board with game pieces

Rendering the Game Board

The last part of the project is to render an image of the game board. The rendered image will be the finished concept art. Before the board can be rendered, however, there are a few steps you need to take to prepare the game board, such as adding a table surface and lights.

1. Pull back from the game board to make space to create a tabletop, as shown in Figure A.33.

2. Create a single-face polygon plane that is 64 units by 64 units, as shown in Figure A.34.

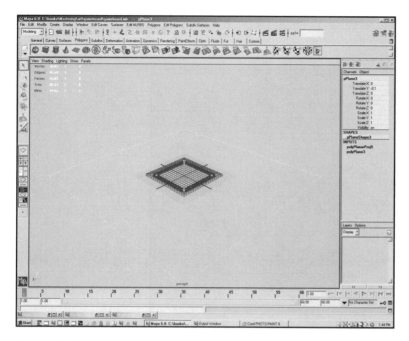

Figure A.33
Pull back from the game board.

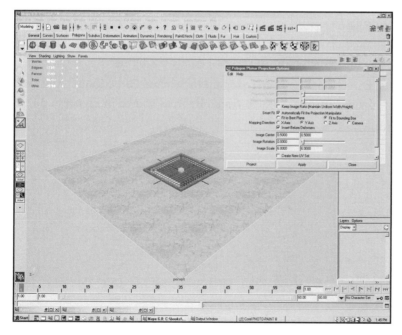

Figure A.34
Create a 64 × 64 polygon plane.

3. Apply the table material to the polygon plane with the projection settings shown in Figure A.35.

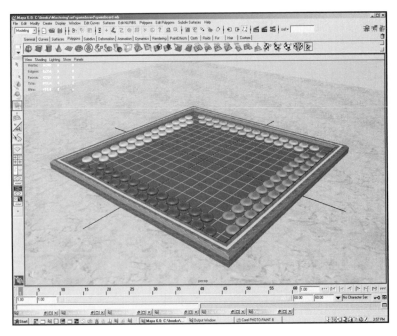

Figure A.35
Apply the table material to the polygon plane.

4. Now zoom in closer to the game board so you can create the lights.

5. Select Create, Lights, Directional Light to bring up the Create Directional Light Options dialog box so you can create a directional light, as shown in Figure A.36.

6. Set the options as shown in Figure A.37.

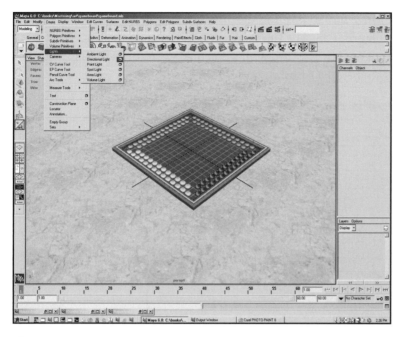

Figure A.36
Bring up the Create Directional Light Options dialog box.

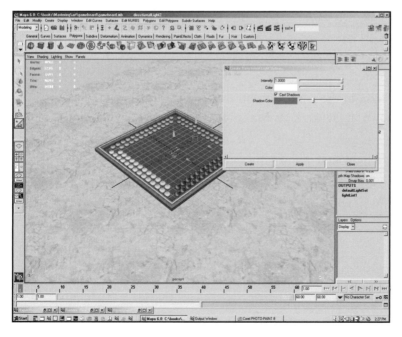

Figure A.37
Set the options for a directional light.

7. Use the Interactive Move tool to position the directional light above the game board, as shown in Figure A.38. The Interactive Move tool is on the left side of the screen. It is represented by the icon with a diagonal slash through it. In Figure A.38, the tool is highlighted by a box around the icon.

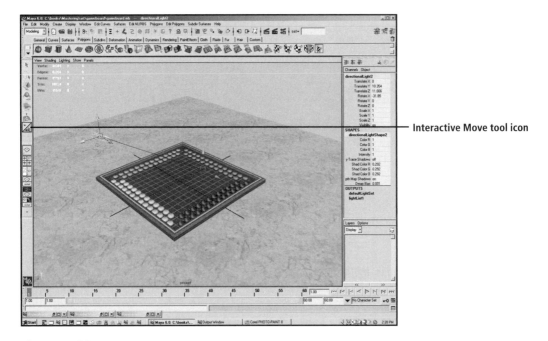

Interactive Move tool icon

Figure A.38
The Interactive Move tool icon has a diagonal slash through it.

8. Create an ambient light in the same way you created the directional light. Use the settings shown in Figure A.39. Make sure the Cast Shadows option is turned off.

9. Position the ambient light so it is above the game board.

10. Position the view in Perspective view for rendering. Figure A.40 shows a good position for the view.

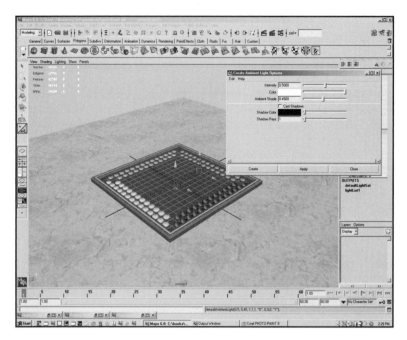

Figure A.39
Set the ambient light to an intensity of 0.5.

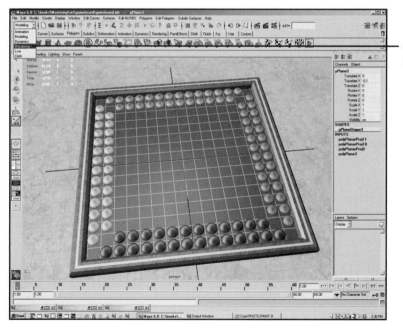

Change to the
Rendering menu set.

Figure A.40
Position the view for rendering.

11. Figure A.40 also shows how to change the main menu to the Rendering menu set. Use the menu in the upper-left corner, as shown.

12. Select Render Current Frame from the Render menu, as shown in Figure A.41.

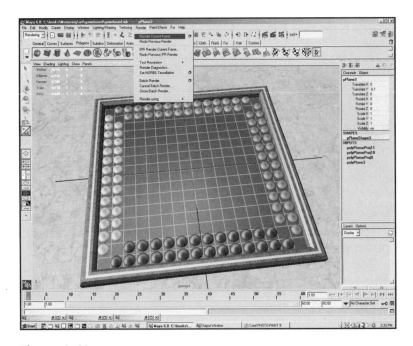

Figure A.41
Select Render Current Frame.

13. The Render View window will appear, as shown in Figure A.42. The Render View window shows the progress of the render.

14. The rendering options are in the Render Global Settings dialog box. Call up the dialog box by selecting Render Globals from the Options menu in the Render View window, as shown in Figure A.43.

Figure A.42
The Render View window shows the progress of the render.

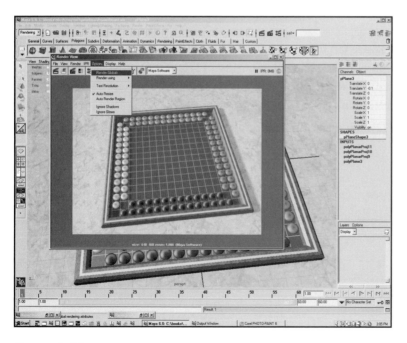

Figure A.43
Bring up the Render Global Settings dialog box.

15. Change the resolution presets to 1k Square, as shown in Figure A.44.

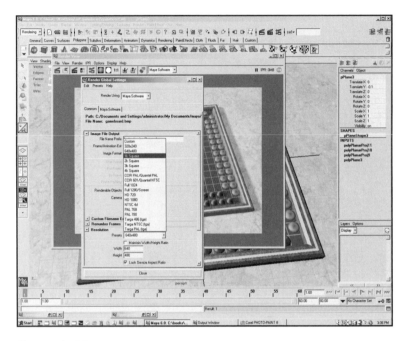

Figure A.44
Set the resolution to 1k Square.

16. Go to the Maya Software tab in the Render Global Settings dialog box. Set the quality to Production and the edge anti-aliasing to Highest Quality, as shown in Figure A.45. This will cause the image to take longer to render, but it will give the final rendering a better look.

17. Render the scene again by selecting Render, Render, Current (Persp), as shown in Figure A.46.

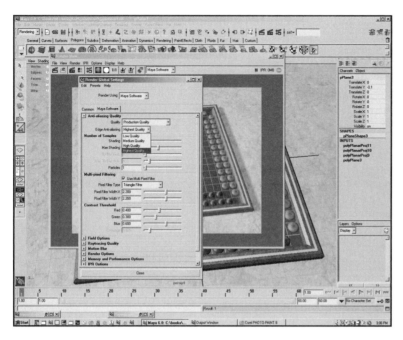

Figure A.45
Set the anti-aliasing quality to the highest available.

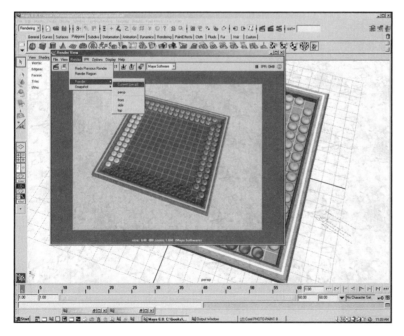

Figure A.46
Render the scene again with the new options.

The finished rendering of the game board should look similar to Figure A.47.

Figure A.47
The rendering of the game board

Because the game board is in 3D, there are many options available to the artist. You can change the view of the board, as shown in Figure A.48.

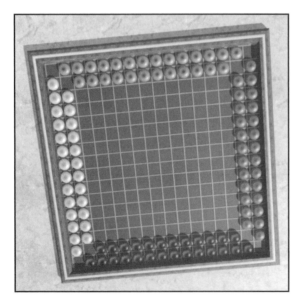

Figure A.48
The board can be seen from different views.

You also can change the lighting, as shown in Figure A.49.

Figure A.49
The lighting can be changed.

And you can view the board with the game pieces moved, as shown in Figure A.50.

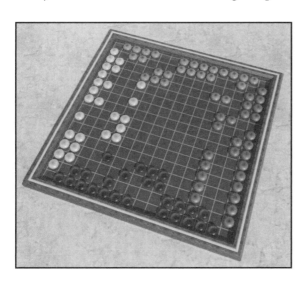

Figure A.50
The game pieces can be moved.

As you can see, having the art in 3D opens up many creative opportunities for the artist. It takes longer to create a 3D model for concept art, but sometimes the effort is worth the trouble.

INDEX

3D models
  advantages of, 172
  male character design, 176–178
  model sheets, 11, 174–175
  templates for, 180–181
3D programs, Maya, game board options
  building, 233–237
  game pieces, adding, 250–254
  rendering, 254–265
  texturing, 239–250

A

actions
  non-player, 59
  sequences, storyboarding, 67–68
Adobe Illustrator drawing program, 102
adventure games
  non-player characters, 135
  player characters, 134
aerial perspective, 128
AI (artificial intelligence)
  non-play actions, 59
  quick character sketches, 133
airbrush painting techniques, 156–161
ambient lights, game boards, 256–257
analogous colors, 122–123
animation
  model sheets and, 171
  storyboarding, 58

arms
  female character design, 179–180
  male character design, 176–178
arrows, in camera action, 62–63
artificial intelligence (AI)
  non-player actions, 59
  quick character sketches, 133
asset count determination, level layout, 98
asset lists, design documents, 212
Attribute Editor (Maya 3D program), 237

B

back story, design documents, 212
background elements, environment illustrations, 124, 126
balance, storyboard drawing skills, 78, 80–81
base model sheets, 181–184
Bates, Bob (*Game Design: The Art and Business of Creating Games*)**, 212**
blank storyboard example, 59
body drawings, full figure, quick character sketches, 140–144
brainstorming, character design, 136
branching charts, game layout charts, 22
bubble examples, water motif, 19–20
budgets
  asset count determination, 98
  design documents, 212
  storyboard uses, 55
buttons, 195

C

camera directions, in storyboarding
arrows, 62–63
close-up shots, 61
pan, 62–63
reversing, 61–62
truck action, 61–62
wide shots, 61
zoom action, 61–63

characters
character illustrations
airbrush painting, 156–161
character templates, 154
detailed example, 162–168
good design elements, 155
as inspirational piece, 154
oil painting techniques, 162–168
overview, 153
simple design examples, 155–162
uses and purpose of, 154
design basics, 8–9
detail levels, 9
female character design, 178–180
game layout charts, 23
ideas for, brainstorming, 136
identification, numbered lists, 106–107
jumping distance, level layout considerations, 95–96
male character design, 176–178
model sheets
base, 181–184
color in, 184
color usage, 173–175
comic book industry use, 172
female characters, 178–180
industries using, 171–172
isometric views, 172
male character design, 176–178
orthogonal views, 173
template creation, 180–181
uses and purpose of, 171–173
placement considerations, 99
quick character sketches
artificial intelligence, 133
character exaggeration, 144–146
enemies, 135–136
full figure drawings, 140–144

head construction, 138–140
non-human characters, 146–148
non-player characters, 135
player characters, 134–135
reasons for, 137–138
shading, 143
standing characters, 140–144
templates, 154
thumbnail sketches, 48–50

charts
complex games and, 35
game layout charts
advantages of, 17
branching charts, 22
character creation, 23
example of, 2
high-score screen, 25
legal screens, 20
load game feature, 22
loading screens, 20–21
main menu, 20
new game option, 22
play game options, 23
player preferences, 23
purpose, 3
quit game option, 25
save game options, 23–24
style design, 17–19
text box frames, 19
title creation, 19
title screens, 20
win/loss options, 23–24
level layout charts
asset count determination, 98
character and object placement considerations, 99
compositional balance, 100
event placement, 99
floor plan example, 101–107
legends, 98
level descriptions, 26–30
level design, 96–97
linear progression formats, 30
overview, 6–7, 95
paths, defining, 99–100
shading examples, 105
story definition, 99

cheekbones, human head sketches, 139
cinematic sequencing, storyboards, 4–5, 57–58
close-up shots, camera direction, 61
clothing, quick character sketches, 142
colors
    aerial perspective, 128
    analogous, 122–123
    color wheel techniques, 120–122
    complimentary, 122
    lighting effects, 118–120
    in model sheets, 173–175, 184
    primary, 120–121
    secondary, 120–121
comic book industries, model sheet use, 172
communication enhancement, storyboards for, 56
complex tasks
    charting considerations, 35
    storyboarding for, 58
complimentary colors, 122
composition techniques
    environment illustrations, 114–115
    level layout, 100
    storyboarding drawing skills, 78
concept art, design basics, 12–13
CorelDRAW drawing program, 102
cover design, 215–216
Create Directional Light Options dialog box, 256
Create Render Node dialog box, 242
credit screens, 193
Croft, Lara (Tomb Raider), 88
crosshatch stroke, pencil drawings, 45
curves, drawing, 46

D
deficient light, 119–120
description area, storyboards, 60
design basics
    character design, 8–9
    concept art, 12–13
    cover design, 215–216
    environment illustrations, 7
    full open approach, 33–34
    game layout charts, 2–3
    GUI (Graphical User Interface), 11–12
    level layouts, 6–7

model sheets, 10
navigation design example, 200–204
open level design, 31–32
open path approach, 32
storyboards
    cinematic sequencing, 4–5
    event outcomes, 4
    navigation techniques, 4
    overview, 3
title pages, 217–218
design documents
    cover design, 215–216
    dummy layouts, 222
    electronic, 215
    font selection, 219–221
    page layout
        diagonal style, 224
        dummy layout, 222
        flush style, 226
        formal style, 223
        special page layout considerations, 229
        staggered style, 225
        styles, 222
        two-column flush style, 227
        two-column random style, 228
    as promotion tool, 213
    as repository tool, 212
    as roadmap, 212
    theme development, 213–214
    title page design, 217–218
    uses and purpose of, 211–213
details, in environment illustrations, 116–118
development
    themes, 213–214
development, themes, 213–214
diagonal layout style, 224
dialog boxes
    Create Directional Light Options, 256
    Create Render Node, 242
    Polygon Plane Options, 233
    Polygon Sphere Options, 250
    Render Global Settings, 260
digital drawing programs, 90
directional lights, game boards, 256–257
directional strokes, pencil drawings, 44–45

documents, design
cover design, 215–216
dummy layouts, 222
electronic, 215
font selection, 219–221
page layout
diagonal style, 224
dummy layout, 222
flush style, 226
formal style, 223
special page layout considerations, 229
staggered style, 225
styles, 222
two-column flush style, 227
two-column random style, 228
as promotion tool, 213
as repository tool, 212
as roadmap, 212
theme development, 213–214
title page design, 217–218
uses and purpose of, 211–213
drawing
characters, quick sketches
artificial intelligence, 133
character exaggeration, 144–146
enemies, 135–136
full figure drawings, 140–144
head construction, 138–140
non-human characters, 146–148
non-player characters, 135
overview, 137
player characters, 134–135
reasons for, 137–138
shading, 143
standing characters, 140–144
components, 39
curves, 46
digital drawing programs, 90
light outlines, 46
loose, 42
original sketches, copying, 49
paper texture considerations, 40–41
pencil drawings
crosshatch stroke, 45
directional strokes, 44–45
hard *versus* soft graphite use, 41–42

object description strokes, 45
scrubbing motion strokes, 44
zigzag strokes, 44
quick sketching, 47, 50–51
renderings, 42
in storyboards
balance considerations, 78, 80–81
composition guidelines, 78
discussed, 71
early sketch examples, 88
eraser damage, 90
focal point techniques, 81–84
pathways, 84
perspective representation, 72–77
shading, 84–87
stages of, 88–92
straight edges, 46
tight, 42
vector-drawing programs, 200

E
ears, human head sketches, 139
ease-in, written directions, 65
ease-out, written directions, 65
edges, game board building techniques, 235–238
electronic game documents, 215
enemies, non-player-controlled characters, 135–136
environment illustrations
background elements, 124, 126
color in
color wheel techniques, 120–122
lighting effects, 118–120
composition techniques, 114–115
defined, 111
design basics, 7
details in, 116–118
for directional focus, 112–113
focal point techniques, 128–129
foreground elements, 126
as inspirational piece, 112
roughed-in drawing example, 113, 123
uses and purposes of, 111–113
eraser damage, 90
event placement, level layout, 99
exaggeration, quick character sketches, 144–145
eyes, human head sketches, 139

F

faces, human head sketches, 139–140
female character design, 178–180
fighting games
  enemy characters, 136
  player characters, 134
flat tone painting techniques, 165–166
flight simulators, concept art, 12
floor plan example, level layout, 101–107
flush layout style, 226
FMVs (Full Motion Videos), 20
focal area, HUD, 198
focal point techniques
  environment illustrations, 128–129
  storyboard drawing skills, 81–84
fog, aerial perspective example, 128
font selection, 219–221
foreground elements, environment illustrations, 126
formal balance, storyboard drawing skills, 80
formal layout style, 223
frame number box, storyboards, 60
fulcrum lever, balance, 80–81
full figure drawings, quick character sketches, 140–144
Full Motion Videos (FMVs), 20
full open approach, level design, 33–34

G

game board (Maya 3D game program)
  building, 233–237
  edges, 235–238
  lights, 256–259
  material attributes, 239
  panels, 233
  planes, 233
  render node creation, 242
  rendering options, 260–264
  shading, 244
  side views, 248
  spheres, 250
  table tops, 254–256
  woodgold material, 246
Game Design: The Art and Business of Creating Games (Bob Bates), 212
game layout charts
  advantages of, 17
  branching charts, 22
  character creation, 23
  example of, 2
  high-score screen, 25
  legal screens, 20
  load game feature, 22
  loading screens, 20–21
  main menu, 20
  new game option, 22
  play game options, 23
  player preferences, 23
  purpose of, 3
  quit game option, 25
  save game options, 23–24
  style design, 17–19
  text box frames, 19
  title creation, 19
  title screens, 20
  win/loss options, 23–24
games
  adventure games
    non-player characters, 135
    player characters, 134
  complex
    storyboarding for, 58
  fighting
    enemy characters, 136
    player characters, 134
  linear, 100
  multiplayer, 134
  open path, 100
  pieces, game board creation, 250–254
  puzzles, 12
  racing
    concept art, 12
    HUD design example, 204–209
    level layout for, 97
  role-playing, 12
  third-person, 88
  Tomb Raider, 88
graphical user interface (GUI)
  buttons, 195
  credit screens, 193
  high-score screens, 193
  HUD (heads-up display), 12
  icons, 196–197

graphical user interface (GUI) *(continued)*
information screens, 189–190
legal screens, 192
level screens, 192–193
loading screens, 191
lose screens, 193
menu lists, 195
menus, 194–197
objects, 197
onscreen displays, 197–200
overview, 11
title screens, 190–191
win screens, 193
graphite considerations, pencil drawings, 41–42
GUI (graphical user interface)
buttons, 195
credit screens, 193
high-score screens, 193
HUD (heads-up display), 12
icons, 196–197
information screens, 189–190
legal screens, 192
level screens, 192–193
loading screens, 191
lose screens, 193
menu lists, 195
menus, 194–197
objects, 197
onscreen displays, 197–200
overview, 11
title screens, 190–191
win screens, 193

H

hair, human head sketches, 139
hard *versus* **soft graphite, pencil drawings, 41–42**
head construction, quick character sketches, 138–140
heads-up display (HUD)
discussed, 197–200
focal area, 198
onscreen elements, creating, 204–209
overview, 12
high-score screen
defined, 193
game layout charts, 25

horizontal lines, linear perspective, 72–74
HUD (heads-up display)
discussed, 197–200
focal area, 198
onscreen elements, creating, 204–209
overview, 12
Hypershade Editor (Maya 3D program), 237

I

icons, 196–197
ideas, character design, 136
identification, numbered lists as, 106–107
illustrations, characters
airbrush painting, 156–161
detailed example, 162–168
good design elements, 155
as inspirational piece, 154
oil painting techniques, 162–168
overview, 153
simple design examples, 155–162
templates, 154
uses and purpose of, 154
images, loading, game board texture, 242
information screens, 189–190
inspiration
character illustrations as, 154
environment illustrations as, 112
Interactive Move tool (Maya 3D game program), 256
isometric views, 172

J

jaw lines, human head sketches, 138
jumping distances, level layout considerations, 95–96

L

Lara Croft, *Tomb Raider,* **88**
large drawing-area panels, storyboarding, 67
layout, page layout
diagonal style, 224
dummy layout, 222
flush style, 226
formal style, 223
special page layout considerations, 229
staggered style, 225
styles, 222

two-column flush style, 227
two-column random style, 228
layout charts. *See* **game layout charts;
    level layout charts**
legal screens
    game layout charts, 20
    uses and purpose of, 192
legends, level layout, 98
level layout charts
    asset count determination, 98
    character and object placement
        considerations, 99
    compositional balance, 100
    event placement, 99
    floor plan example, 101–107
    legends, 98
    level descriptions, 26–30
    level design, 96–97
    linear progression formats, 30
    overview, 6–7, 95
    paths, defining, 99–100
    shading examples, 105
    story definition, 99
level screens, 192–193
levels
    defined, 6
    full open approach, 33–34
    open level design, 31–32
    open path approach, 32
    replay value, 31
light outlines, drawings, 46
lighting
    aerial perspective, 128
    color effects, 118–120
    deficient light, 119–120
    pure, 119
    reflected, 119
    visible band of light, 119
    white light, 119
lights, game boards, 256–259
linear games, 100
linear perspective representation
    horizontal lines, 72–74
    single-point perspective, 74–75
    three-point perspective, 77–78
    two-point perspective, 74–76
    vanishing point, 74–75

linear progression formats, 30
load game feature, game layout charts, 22
loading images, game board texture, 242
loading screens
    game layout charts, 20–21
    uses and purpose of, 191
loose drawing, 42
lose screens, 193

M

magical characters, non-human, 146–148
main menu, game layout charts, 20
male character design, 176–178
material attributes, game board texture, 239
Maya 3D program, game board techniques
    building, 233–237
    game pieces, adding, 250–254
    rendering, 254–265
    texturing, 239–250
menu lists, 195
menus, 194–197
model sheets
    base, 181–184
    color in, 184
    color use, 173–175
    comic book industry use, 172
    female characters, 178–180
    industries using, 171–172
    isometric views, 172
    male character design, 176–178
    orthogonal views, 173
    template creation, 180–181
    uses and purpose of, 171–173
    uses for, 10
mouth, human head sketches, 139
multiplayer games, player characters, 134

N

navigation techniques
    navigation design example, 200–204
    storyboards, 4
neck, human head sketches, 139
new game option, game layout charts, 22
**non-human characters, quick character sketches,
    146–148**
non-player actions, 59

non-player characters, 135
nose, human head sketches, 138–139
numbered lists, as identification option, 106–107

O

objects
GUI, 197
replicating, 102
observation, good character design, 136
oil painting techniques, 162–168
onscreen displays, 197–200
open level design, 31–32
open path approach, level design, 32
open path games, 100
orthogonal views, 173

P

page layout
diagonal style, 224
dummy layout, 222
flush style, 226
formal style, 223
special page layout considerations, 229
staggered style, 225
styles, 222
two-column flush style, 227
two-column random style, 228
painting techniques
aerial perspective, 128
airbrush, 156–161
flat tones, 165–166
oil paint, 162–168
pan camera action, 62–63
panel numbers, storyboards, 60
panels, game board building techniques, 233
paper texture considerations
drawing and, 40–41
eraser damage, 90
tracing paper, 176, 181
paths
level layout considerations, 99–100
open path games, 100
pathways, storyboard drawing techniques, 84
pencil drawings
crosshatch stroke, 45
directional strokes, 44–45

hard *versus* soft graphite use, 41–42
object description strokes, 45
scrubbing motion strokes, 44
zigzag strokes, 44
perspective representation, linear perspective, 72–77
picture area, storyboards, 60
placement considerations
characters, 99
events, 99
Planar Mapping tool (Maya 3D program), 252
planes, game board building techniques, 233
planning stages, storyboards and, 55–56
play game option, game layout charts, 23
player characters, 134–135
player preferences, game layout charts, 23
players, non-player actions, 59
Polygon Plane Options dialog box, 233
Polygon Sphere Options dialog box, 250
primary colors, 120–121
problem solving, storyboards for, 57
production charts, design documents, 212
progression
linear progression formats, 32
story, 32
promotion tool, design documents as, 213
pure lighting, 119
puzzle games, 12

Q

quit game option, game layout charts, 25

R

racing games
concept art, 12
HUD design example, 204–209
level layout for, 97
rainbows, visible light example, 119
readability, font selection, 219–220
references, renderings, 42
reflected light, 119
Render Global Settings dialog box, 260
render node creation, game boards, 242
rendering options, game boards, 260–264
renderings, drawing techniques, 42
replay value, 31

replicating objects, 102
role-playing games, 12

S

sans serif fonts, 220
save game options, game layout charts, 23–24
Scale tool (Maya 3D program), 237
scene box, storyboards, 60
scores, high-score screens, 25, 193
screens
    credit, 193
    high-score, 193
    information, 189–190
    legal, 192
    level, 192–193
    loading, 191
    lose, 193
    screen elements, water motif, 20
    title, 190–191
    win, 193
scrubbing motion strokes, pencil drawings, 44
secondary colors, 120–121
sequencing, level layout charts, 26–30
serif fonts, 220
shading methods
    game board texture, 244
    level layout, 105
    light to dark variations, 84
    natural paths of movement, 85
    pencil drawings, 44–45
    quick character sketches, 143
    smooth, 244–245
    storyboard drawing techniques, 84–87
    value sketches, 86
shapes, 200–204
side views, game board texture, 248
single-point perspective, linear perspective
    representation, 74–75
sketching. *See* drawing
skill progression, 32
smooth shading methods, 244–245
soft *versus* hard graphite, pencil drawings, 41–42
special-use panels, storyboarding, 65–67
spheres
    game board pieces, 250

human head construction, quick character
    sketches, 138–139
staggered layout style, 225
standing characters, quick character sketches,
    140–144
story definition, level layout, 99
story progression, 32
storyboards
    action sequences, 67–68
    animation sequences, 58
    blank example, 59
    camera directions, 61–64
    cinematic sequencing, 4–5, 57–58
    for communication enhancement, 56
    for complex tasks, 58
    description area, 60
    drawing skills
        balance considerations, 78, 80–81
        composition guidelines, 78
        discussed, 71
        early sketch examples, 88
        eraser damage, 90
        focal point techniques, 81–84
        pathways, 84
        perspective representation, 72–77
        shading, 84–87
        stages of, 88–92
    event outcomes, 4
    frame number box, 60
    importance of, 59
    large drawing-area panel, 67
    navigation techniques, 4
    non-player actions, 59
    overview, 3
    panel numbers, 60
    picture area, 60
    planning stages, 55–56
    for problem solving, 57
    reasons for, 55–59
    scene box, 60
    special-use panels, 65–67
    vertical panels, 66
    wide panels, 65–66
    written directions, 65
straight edges, thumbnail sketches, 46

styles
  font selection considerations, 219–220
  page layout, 222
  style design, game layout charts, 17–19
symbols, 103

T

tabletops, game boards, 254–256
task lists, design documents, 212
templates
  3D models, 180–181
  character, 154
  model sheets, 180–181
terrain elements, 6–7
text box frames, layout charts, 19
themes, developing, 213–214
third-person games, 88
three-point perspective, linear perspective
  representation, 77–78
thumbnail sketches
  character thumbnails, 48–50
  curves in, 46
  drawing components, 39
  examples of, 43
  light outlines, 46
  loose drawing, 42
  original sketches, copying, 49
  paper texture considerations, 40–41
  pencil drawings, 41–42
  pencil strokes, 44–45
  quick sketching, 47, 50–51
  renderings, 42
  straight edges, 46
  tight drawing, 42
  value sketches, 86
tight drawing, 42
title screens
  game layout charts, 20
  uses and purpose of, 190–191

titles
  creating, game layout charts, 19
  title page design, 217–218
Tomb Raider, **88**
tooth, drawing surface considerations, 41
tracing paper, 176, 181
trademarks, character design, 9
truck action, camera direction, 61–62
two-column flush layout style, 227
two-column random layout style, 228
two-point perspective, linear perspective
  representation, 74–76

U

user interface, 4

V

value, focal point techniques, 82
value sketches, 86
vanishing point, linear perspective representation,
  74–75
vector-drawing programs, 200
vertical panels, storyboarding, 66
visible band of light, 119
visual enhancement, title page design, 217–218

W

water motif example
  game layout charts, 17–25
  level layout charts, 26–30
white light, 119
wide panels, storyboarding, 65–66
wide shots, camera direction, 61
win/loss options, game layout charts, 23–24
win screens, 193
woodgold material, game board texture, 246
written directions, storyboarding, 65

Z

zigzag strokes, pencil drawings, 44
zoom action, camera direction, 61–63

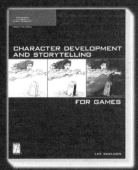

License Agreement/Notice of Limited Warranty